AIR FRYER COOKBOOK FOR BEGINNERS

2100 Days of Delectable and Effortless Home Cooking. Discover Fast, Flavorful Air fryer Recipes with Foolproof Instructions!

LARISSA H. BARTON

AIR FRYER COOKBOOK FOR BEGINNERS

AIR FRYER COOKBOOK FOR BEGINNERS

LARISSA H. BARTON

No part of this book may be reproduced in any form or by any electronic or mechanical means, including photocopying, recording, or by any information storage and retrieval system now known or hereafter invented, without written permission from the publisher. The only exception is by a reviewer, who may quote short excerpts in a published review.

This document is aimed to provide accurate and reliable information in the light if the selected topic and all covered issues. This book is sold with the ideas that the publisher is not required to render an officially permitted, accounting, or otherwise, qualified services. If advice is required in any way, professional or legal, seasoned experts of the profession should be consulted

Every information given herein is claimed to be consistent and truthful, in case of any liability, with regard to inattention or otherwise, by any use or abuse of processes, policies, or directions contained within is solely the responsibility of the recipient reader. Under no conditions will any blame or legal responsibility be held against the publishers for any damages, monetary loss or reparation, due to the information herein.

The information herein is provided entirely for informational purposes, and it is universal. The information is provided without any type of guarantee assurance or a contract. The trademarks that are used within the document are without any consent, and the publication of the trademark is without the backing of the trademark owner or any support. All brands and trademarks used within this book are to clarify the text only, and they are owned by their owners, not affiliated with this publication. Respective authors of this publication own all copyrights not help by the publisher.

Copyright © LARISSA H. BARTON

AIR FRYER COOKBOOK FOR BEGINNERS

TABLE OF CONTENTS

- INTRODUCTION 11
  - WHAT IS AN AIR FRYER? 11
  - HOW DOES AN AIR FRYER WORK? 11
  - BENEFITS OF USING AN AIR FRYER 12
  - TYPES OF AIR FRYERS 12
- PART ONE 16
  - SETTING UP YOUR AIR FRYER 16
  - ESSENTIAL ACCESSORIES FOR YOUR AIR FRYER 16
  - GROCERY LIST 17
- PART TWO 19
  - MAIN DISHES 19
  - 1. AIR FRYER BBQ RIBS 19
  - 2. AIR FRYER BEEF AND BROCCOLI STIR FRY 20
  - 3. AIR FRYER BEEF KEBABS ... 21
  - 4. AIR FRYER BEEF STIR FRY . 22
  - 5. AIR FRYER CHICKEN FAJITAS 24
  - 6. AIR FRYER CHICKEN PARMESAN 24
  - 7. AIR FRYER CHICKEN WINGS 26
  - 8. AIR FRYER FISH AND CHIPS 26
  - 9. AIR FRYER FRIED CHICKEN 28
  - 10. AIR FRYER MEATLOAF 29
  - 11. AIR FRYER PORK CHOPS . 30
  - 12. AIR FRYER PORK TENDERLOIN 31
  - 13. AIR FRYER QUICHE 32
  - 14. AIR FRYER ROASTED TURKEY BREAST 33
  - 15. AIR FRYER SALMON WITH LEMON AND HERBS 34
  - 16. AIR FRYER SAUSAGE AND PEPPERS 35
  - 17. AIR FRYER SHRIMP SCAMPI 36
  - 18. AIR FRYER STUFFED BELL PEPPERS 37
  - 19. AIR FRYER TOFU AND VEGETABLE STIR FRY 38
  - 20. AIR FRYER VEGGIE BURGERS 39

21. AIR FRYER BUFFALO CAULIFLOWER BITES 40
22. AIR FRYER GRILLED CHEESE SANDWICH 42
23. AIR FRYER STEAK 43
24. AIR FRYER SWEET POTATO FRIES 44
25. AIR FRYER ZUCCHINI FRITTERS 45
PART THREE 46
APPETIZERS AND SNACKS 46
1. AIR FRYER AVOCADO FRIES 46
2. AIR FRYER BACON-WRAPPED JALAPENOS 47
3. CRISPY AIR FRYER CHICKPEAS 48
4. AIR FRYER CHEESY GARLIC BREAD 49
5. AIR FRYER EGG ROLLS 50
6. AIR FRYER FALAFEL 51
7. AIR FRYER FRENCH TOAST STICKS 52
8. AIR FRYER FRIED PICKLES . 53
9. AIR FRYER CRAB RANGOON 54
10. AIR FRYER MOZZARELLA STICKS 55
11. AIR FRYER ONION RINGS 56
12. AIR FRYER PARMESAN ZUCCHINI COINS 57
13. AIR FRYER PIZZA ROLLS .. 58
14. AIR FRYER PANKO CRUSTED SHRIMP 59
15. AIR FRYER PORK RINDS .. 60
16. AIR FRYER SWEET POTATO FRIES 61
17. AIR FRYER TOASTED RAVIOLI 62
18. AIR FRYER VEGETABLE SPRING ROLLS 63
19. AIR-FRIED COCONUT SHRIMP 65
20. AIR FRYER BUFFALO CHICKEN DIP 66
PART FOUR 68
SIDES AND VEGETABLES 68
1. AIR FRYER ASPARAGUS 68

AIR FRYER COOKBOOK FOR BEGINNERS

2. AIR FRYER BAKED SWEET POTATOES 69

3. AIR FRYER CARROT FRIES . 70

4. AIR FRYER CAULIFLOWER RICE 71

5. AIR FRYER CORN ON THE COB 72

6. AIR FRYER GARLIC ROASTED POTATOES 73

7. AIR FRYER GRILLED VEGETABLES 74

8. AIR FRYER MAC AND CHEESE BITES 75

9. AIR FRYER PARMESAN ROASTED BROCCOLI 76

10. AIR FRYER POTATO WEDGES 77

11. AIR FRYER ROASTED BUTTERNUT SQUASH 78

12. AIR FRYER ROASTED CARROTS 79

13. AIR FRYER ROASTED EGGPLANT 80

14. AIR FRYER ROASTED GARLIC 81

15. AIR FRYER ROASTED GREEN BEANS 82

16. AIR FRYER SWEET POTATO COINS 83

17. AIR FRYER TATER TOTS ... 84

19. AIR FRYER ZUCCHINI CHIPS 86

20. AIR FRYER ROASTED CAULIFLOWER 87

PART FIVE 89

DESSERTS 89

1. AIR FRYER APPLE CHIPS 89

2. AIR FRYER APPLE PIE BITES 90

3. AIR FRYER BANANA BREAD 91

4. AIR FRYER BLUEBERRY MUFFINS 92

5. AIR FRYER BROWNIES 93

6. AIR FRYER CARROT CAKE .. 94

7. AIR FRYER CINNAMON ROLLS 95

8. AIR FRYER FRUIT TARTS 96

9. AIR FRYER FUNNEL CAKES 97

10. AIR FRYER GRILLED PEACHES 98
11. AIR FRYER POUND CAKE 99
12. AIR FRYER PUMPKIN MUFFINS 100
13. AIR FRYER S'MORES 101
14. AIR FRYER STRAWBERRY TURNOVERS 102
15. AIR FRYER SWEET POTATO PIE 103
16. AIR FRYER VANILLA CUPCAKES 104
17. AIR FRYER WAFFLE BITES 105
18. AIR FRYER WARM CINNAMON APPLES 106
19. AIR FRYER YEAST DONUTS 107
20. AIR FRYER ZUCCHINI BREAD 108

PART SIX 110

TIPS FOR COOKING WITH AN AIR FRYER 110
TROUBLESHOOTING COMMON AIR FRYER ISSUES 110
HOW TO CLEAN AND MAINTAIN YOUR AIR FRYER 112
CONCLUSION 113
PERSONAL REFLECTION 113
MEAL PLAN 114
SAFETY TIPS FOR USING AN AIR FRYER 116
TIPS FOR SUBSTITUTING INGREDIENTS 117
GLOSSARY OF INGREDIENTS AND TERMS 118
GLOSSARY OF COOKING TECHNIQUES 120

INTRODUCTION

WHAT IS AN AIR FRYER?

An air fryer is a kitchen appliance that uses hot air instead of oil to fry, bake, grill, and roast food. It's meant to taste and feel like conventional deep-fried food, but with much less fat and calories. As a result, it is a popular option for people who want to eat better without compromising taste.

An air fryer works by swirling hot air around the food, and evenly frying it on all sides. The food is put in a basket or tray, and the built-in fan circulates hot air around it, crisping it to perfection. The heated air and rapid circulation keep the food from getting greasy and mushy, which is a common issue when cooking using traditional methods. Air fryers come in a range of forms and sizes, but they all have one feature: they're small and simple to use. Most types have a digital display that lets you program the temperature and cooking time, making it easier to achieve consistent results. They're also low-maintenance, with most versions including dishwasher-safe detachable baskets and trays for simple cleaning.

Air fryers have been around for a while, but they've only lately acquired popularity owing to the increased emphasis on healthy eating. They're a great alternative to traditional deep-frying techniques since they let you consume your favorite fried meals without all the extra fat and calories. An air fryer is undoubtedly worth considering whether you want to prepare healthier versions of your favorite snacks or just want a handy method to cook a range of meals.

HOW DOES AN AIR FRYER WORK?

The same as typical deep-frying techniques, but without the extra fat and calories. But how does it operate in practice? Let us investigate more. An air fryer cooks food by using a fan to circulate heated air around the food. The food is put in a basket or tray, and the built-in fan circulates hot air around it, evenly frying it on all sides. The heated air and rapid circulation keep the food from getting greasy and mushy, which is a common issue when cooking using conventional techniques.

The air fryer's heating element creates heat, which is circulated by the blower to create a high-temperature atmosphere. The combination of the high temperature and the flowing hot air lets the food cook rapidly and evenly. Moisture evaporates from the food as it cooks, forming a crispy outer layer that seals in taste and nutrients.

The changeable temperature control of an air fryer is one of its key features. This enables you to customize the temperature for each item, ensuring that it cooks uniformly and to the optimum amount of crispiness. Furthermore, most air fryers have a timer that allows you to control the cooking duration, guaranteeing that your food is always cooked to perfection.

Another significant feature of air fryers is their small size. The majority of types are small and lightweight, making them ideal for storage in even the smallest kitchens. They're also low-maintenance, with most versions including dishwasher-safe detachable baskets and trays for simple cleaning.

BENEFITS OF USING AN AIR FRYER

An air fryer offers several advantages, from crispy fried chicken to flawlessly roasted veggies that makes it a must-have piece of equipment in every kitchen. Let's take a deeper look at some of the most important benefits of using an air fryer. One of the most significant benefits of owning an air fryer is that it enables you to prepare your favorite fried meals without all of the extra oil and calories. Air fryers are very adaptable and may be used to prepare a broad variety of foods, from fried chicken and fish to roasted vegetables and baked products. You can prepare a variety of foods with ease because of its adjustable temperature control and timer, making it a useful addition to any kitchen. It's also ideal for individuals with limited kitchen space since its small and simple to store.

It is fast and simple to operate. Simply put your food in the basket or tray, adjust the temperature and timer, and let the air fryer handle the rest. The built-in fan circulates hot air over the food, evenly frying it on all sides, and the timer guarantees that your food is always cooked to perfection. Crispy and delicious results: Crispy and delicious results are one of the key reasons why people love air fryers. It generates a high-temperature atmosphere that seals in taste and nutrients by circulating hot air around the food, resulting in crispy and tasty foods every time. An air fryer will dazzle whether you're cooking fried chicken, roasted veggies, or baked goodies. Air fryers are very simple to maintain. Most versions have dishwasher-safe detachable baskets and trays, making cleanup a breeze after cooking. There's also no need to be concerned about messy spills or tough stains since there's no oil involved.

TYPES OF AIR FRYERS

Air fryers have grown in popularity in recent years, and with that growth came an increase in the number of alternatives available on the market. There is an air fryer to meet everyone's needs, from smaller versions for small kitchens to bigger, more feature-packed ones for larger families. Let's take a deeper look at some of the many varieties of air fryers on the market. Compact air fryers: Compact air fryers are ideal for people with limited kitchen space or who want a quick method to prepare smaller dishes. These types are often lower in capacity and are meant to be compact and lightweight, making them easier to store when not in use. They're also ideal for singles, couples, or small families looking for a fast and simple method to prepare decent meals.

Large-capacity air fryers: Large-capacity air fryers are ideal for people with a larger family or who often entertain guests. These versions often have a greater capacity, letting you prepare larger dishes, and are frequently outfitted with extra amenities like as several cooking trays and a digital display. They're also ideal for folks who enjoy preparing multi-course dinners. Multi-functional air fryers: For those searching for a flexible appliance that can perform many culinary duties, multi-functional air fryers are an excellent choice. These versions often have other attachments, such as baking pans and roasting trays, enabling you to easily prepare a range of cuisines. They're also a good option for those who want a single device to replace various kitchen equipment, such as a toaster oven and a deep fryer.

Smart air fryers: Smart air fryers are great for those looking for an air fryer that is linked to their smart home system. These versions often have built-in Wi-Fi, letting you manage and monitor the cooking process from your smartphone or tablet. They're also a good option for people searching for an air fryer that's simple to operate, with straightforward touch controls and preset cooking settings.

LARISSA H. BARTON

LET'S GET STARTED

PART ONE
SETTING UP YOUR AIR FRYER

It may seem overwhelming to set up your air fryer for the first time, but it is really fairly easy. You'll be up and cooking in no time with just a few simple steps! Here's a step-by-step guide to getting you started.

- **Unbox and Assemble your Air Fryer**

The first step in assembling and unboxing your air fryer is to unpack it. Most air fryers come with many elements that must be installed, including the basket, drip tray, and control panel. It is critical to follow the directions in the handbook to ensure that your air fryer is correctly assembled and works correctly.

- **Clean the Air Fryer**

It is critical to fully clean your air fryer before using it for the first time. Wipe off the basket, drip tray, and any other parts that came into touch with the air fryer during installation using a moist cloth. It's critical to check for residue from the production process since this might damage the flavor and quality of your meal.

- **Adjust the Settings**

After you've assembled and cleaned your air fryer, you'll want to tweak the settings to your preference. Most air fryers include a digital display on which you can regulate the temperature and cooking duration, as well as choose from a number of cooking programs. Take some time to get accustomed to the controls and settings, as this will make future usage of your air fryer simpler.

- **Preheat the Air Fryer**

Preheat your air fryer before starting to cook your meal. This guarantees that your food cooks evenly and with the optimum crispiness. Most air fryers include a preheat setting, so just choose it and adjust the temperature to your liking. Allow a few minutes for the air fryer to warm before you begin cooking.

- **Cook Your Food**

It's time to start frying now that your air fryer has been preheated! Fill the basket with your food, ensuring sure it's fairly distributed and not congested. Set the temperature and cooking time, then turn off the air fryer. It is critical to inspect your food and shake the basket on a regular basis to ensure that it cooks evenly.

ESSENTIAL ACCESSORIES FOR YOUR AIR FRYER

Having the right air fryer accessories can make or break your cooking experience. They not only make it easy to prepare a variety of dishes, but they also help you get the most out of your air fryer. Here are some critical air fryer accessories that every owner should have.

- Basket Dividers for Air Fryer. Basket dividers are a must-have item for every air fryer owner. They let you cook numerous items at the same time without their touching or mingling. This is particularly useful when making a complete dinner since you can cook all of your components in the same basket without worrying about them getting mixed up.

- Air fryer liners are thin sheets of nonstick material that you lay in the bottom of your air fryer basket. They keep food from clinging to the basket, which makes cleanup a snap. They also help to keep your meal crisp since they don't absorb any oil or moisture.

- Skewers for the Air Fryer. Air fryer skewers are ideal for cooking kabobs, shish tawook, and other skewered meals. They're also useful for cooking tiny bits of meat or veggies that might otherwise fall through the basket.

- Air Fryer Rack. An air fryer rack is an excellent addition to frying numerous layers of food at the same time. This is especially helpful for cooking large cuts of meat, as it allows you to cook more in one batch. The rack also raises food away from the basket's bottom, providing consistent cooking.

- Air Fryer Baking Pan. A baking pan for an air fryer is ideal for baking cakes, muffins, and other baked goods. It's designed to fit exactly within the air fryer basket, allowing you to bake just as you would in a regular oven.

- Tongs for Air Fryer: Air fryer tongs are essential for flipping and removing food from the basket. They are heat-resistant and feature a non-slip grip, making them suitable for use in an air fryer.

- Air Fryer Silicone Mats. Similar to air fryer liners, air fryer silicone mats are meant to fit on the bottom of the basket. They're perfect for cooking delicate foods, as they prevent them from sticking to the basket and ensure that they cook evenly.

GROCERY LIST

A grocery list is a must-have tool for anybody who wants to get the most out of their air fryer. Whether you're a seasoned chef or a novice, having a well-stocked pantry and a thorough shopping list will guarantee that you always have the items you need on hand to prepare tasty and healthful meals in your air fryer. Here are some must-have goods for your air fryer shopping list.

- **Vegetables:** A variety of fresh or frozen vegetables should be on every air fryer grocery list. There are several alternatives available, ranging from leafy greens to root veggies. Air frying works well with bell peppers, carrots, zucchini, and broccoli because they cook rapidly and evenly.

- **Meat:** Whether you like chicken, beef, or pork, keeping a range of meats on hand is an excellent way to ensure that you always have a fast and simple meal alternative. Air frying works well with chicken breast, tenderloin, and drumsticks because they cook rapidly and are juicy and tasty.

• **Seafood:** Because it cooks fast and evenly, seafood is an excellent choice for air frying. Shrimp, scallops, and salmon are all great choices for air frying since they cook rapidly while remaining delicate and tasty.

• **Breadcrumbs:** Breadcrumbs are a great ingredient to have on hand for air frying. They're ideal for coating meals to produce a crispy surface, and they're also a tasty addition to panko-crusted chicken or fish recipes.

• **Spices and seasonings:** Keeping a range of spices and seasonings on hand is an excellent way to improve the taste and thrill of your air fryer meals. From dried herbs like basil and oregano to seasoning mixes like Cajun seasoning and chili powder, having a well-stocked pantry of spices and seasonings can guarantee that your air fryer dinners never get dull.

• **Oils:** Oils are necessary for air frying since they help to create a crispy coating on your meal. Because they have a high smoke point and are healthier than other oils, olive oil, avocado oil, and coconut oil are all excellent choices for air frying.

• **Sauces:** Having a selection of sauces on hand is a terrific way to spice up your air fryer dishes. There is a sauce for every taste, from barbecue to honey mustard.

• **Frozen Foods:** Because they cook fast and evenly, frozen foods are an excellent choice for air frying. Having a range of frozen meals on hand, from frozen french fries to frozen chicken nuggets, is a terrific way to ensure you have a quick and easy meal option.

• Almonds, cashews, and pecans are excellent for air frying because they get properly toasted and crispy. They make an excellent snack on their own or may be used in other meals to add crunch.

• **Tofu:** Tofu is a high-protein food that may be air-fried for a crispy finish. It's a delicious vegetarian choice for air fryer dinners that may be seasoned to suit.

• Root vegetables, such as potatoes, sweet potatoes, and carrots, are ideal for air frying since they cook rapidly and evenly. They may be served as a side dish or added to other recipes to provide taste and nutrients.

• **Bread:** Air-fried bread with a crispy crust may be used as a basis for sandwiches or as a side dish with dips.

• **Fruit:** Peaches, pineapples, and apples may be air-fried to make a warm, sweet treat. They are a healthier alternative to classic fried treats and may be flavored with cinnamon or other spices.

PART TWO

MAIN DISHES

1. AIR FRYER BBQ RIBS

Ingredients:

- Salt and pepper, to taste

- 1 teaspoon of paprika

- 1 teaspoon of garlic powder

- 1/2 teaspoon of cayenne pepper

- 1 teaspoon of onion powder

- 1 teaspoon of dried thyme

- 1 teaspoon of dried basil

- 1/2 teaspoon of cumin

- 1/2 cup of your favorite BBQ sauce

- 2.5 pounds of baby back pork ribs

Instructions:

- Rinse the ribs and pat dry with paper towels. Remove the membrane from the back of the ribs.

- Season the ribs generously with salt, pepper, paprika, garlic powder, onion powder, thyme, basil, cumin, and cayenne pepper.

- Place the seasoned ribs in the air fryer basket, ensuring they are not overlapping.

- Set the air fryer to 400°F and cook the ribs for 20 minutes.

- After 20 minutes, brush the ribs with the BBQ sauce.

- Boil the ribs for an extra 10 minutes.

- Now, check the internal temperature of the ribs. They should be 145°F or higher.

- Once done, remove the ribs from the air fryer and let them rest for 5 minutes before serving.

Nutritional Information (per serving, based on 4 servings):

- Fat: 38g

- Carbohydrates: 12g

- Calories: 638

- Protein: 63g

- Sodium: 1731mg

2. AIR FRYER BEEF AND BROCCOLI STIR FRY

Ingredients:

- 1 pound of sirloin steak, thinly sliced

- 2 cups of broccoli florets

- 1 red bell pepper, sliced

- 1 green bell pepper, sliced

- 1 yellow onion, sliced

- 2 cloves of garlic, minced

- 2 tablespoons of vegetable oil

- 2 tablespoons of cornstarch

- 2 tablespoons of soy sauce

- 1 tablespoon of hoisin sauce

- 1 tablespoon of honey

- 1 teaspoon of sesame oil

- Salt and pepper, to taste

Instructions:

- In a small bowl, whisk together the cornstarch, soy sauce, hoisin sauce, honey, and sesame oil.

- In the air fryer basket, add the broccoli florets, red bell pepper, green bell pepper, onion, and garlic. Drizzle with 1 tablespoon of vegetable oil and sprinkle with salt and pepper.

- Set the air fryer to 400°F and cook the vegetables for 10 minutes, flipping them halfway through.

- In a separate bowl, toss the sliced sirloin steak with 1 tablespoon of vegetable oil, salt, and pepper.

- Remove the vegetables from the air fryer and place them on a plate.

- Add the seasoned sirloin steak to the air fryer basket and cook for 6-8 minutes or until cooked to your desired degree of doneness.

- In a large pan over high heat, stir fry the cooked vegetables and steak with the sauce mixture until heated through and the sauce has thickened.

- Serve the stir fry over a bed of rice or noodles.

Nutritional Information (per serving, based on 4 servings):- Calories: 521 - Fat: 28g - Protein: 43g

- Sodium: 1097mg

- Carbohydrates: 27g

3. AIR FRYER BEEF KEBABS

Ingredients:

- 1 lb. beef sirloin, cut into 1 1/2-inch cube

- 1 red bell pepper, cut into 1 1/2 inch squares

- 1 yellow onion, cut into 1 1/2 inch squares

- 8 cherry tomatoes

- Salt and pepper to taste

- 1 tsp. garlic powder

- 1 tsp. paprika

- 1 tsp. dried oregano

- 1 tbsp. olive oil

Instructions:

- Preheat your air fryer to 400°F.

In a large bowl, combine the beef cubes, red bell pepper, yellow onion, and cherry tomatoes.

- Add salt and pepper to taste, garlic powder, paprika, dried oregano, and olive oil to the bowl. Mix everything together to make sure that each piece is evenly coated.

- Skewer the beef cubes, bell pepper, onion, and cherry tomatoes, alternating them on each skewer.

- Place the skewered beef kebabs in the air fryer basket, making sure they are not touching each other.

- Air fry the kebabs for 12-15 minutes or until the beef is cooked through and the vegetables are slightly charred. Turn the skewers over halfway through cooking to ensure even cooking.

- Remove the kebabs from the air fryer and let them rest for a few minutes before serving.

- Serve with a side of rice or your favorite dipping sauce.

Nutritional Information: Serves 4 Per serving:

- Cholesterol: 68mg

- Sodium: 216mg

- Total Carbohydrates: 7.3g

- Protein: 26.6g

- Dietary Fiber: 1.9g

- Calories: 238

- Total Fat: 12.6g   - Saturated Fat: 3.6g   - Total Sugars: 3.7g

AIR FRYER COOKBOOK FOR BEGINNERS

4. AIR FRYER BEEF STIR FRY

Ingredients:

- 1 lb beef (sirloin, flank, or round steak), sliced into thin strips

- 1 red bell pepper, sliced

- 1 yellow onion, sliced

- 2 cloves of garlic, minced

- 1 tbsp. fresh ginger, grated

- 1 cup broccoli florets

- 2 tbsp. oil

- 1 tbsp. cornstarch

- 1/4 cup low-sodium soy sauce

- 1 tbsp. brown sugar

- 1 tbsp. rice vinegar

- 1 tsp. sesame oil

Instructions:

- In a small bowl, mix together the cornstarch, soy sauce, brown sugar, rice vinegar, and sesame oil to make the stir-fry sauce. Set aside.

- Set your air fryer to 400°F.

- Now, in your large bowl, toss the sliced beef with 1 tablespoon of oil.

- Add the beef strips to the air fryer basket in a single layer, making sure not to overcrowd the basket. Cook for 5 minutes, then flip the food and cook for an additional 5 minutes.

- Remove the beef from the air fryer and set aside.

- In a large bowl, toss the sliced bell pepper, onion, garlic, ginger, and broccoli with 1 tablespoon of oil.

- Add the vegetables to the air fryer basket in a single layer, making sure not to overcrowd the basket. Cook for 4-5 minutes, then flip and cook for another 4-5 minutes.

- In a large wok or frying pan, heat the remaining oil over high heat. Add the cooked beef and stir fry sauce to the pan and stir to combine. Cook for 2-3 minutes or until the sauce has thickened.

- Add the cooked vegetables to the pan and stir to combine. Keep cooking for 1-2 more minutes.

- Serve the beef stir fry over a bed of rice, garnished with chopped green onions and sesame seeds if desired.

Nutritional Information (per serving, based on 4 servings):

- Fiber: 2g

- Sugar: 9g

- Protein: 29g

- Calories: 360

- Fat: 20g

- Saturated Fat: 5g

- Cholesterol: 80mg

- Sodium: 860mg

- Carbohydrates: 15g

5. AIR FRYER CHICKEN FAJITAS

Ingredients:

- 1 lb boneless, skinless chicken breasts, sliced into thin strips

- One red bell pepper, cut into thin strips

- 1 yellow onion, sliced into thin strips

- 2 cloves garlic, minced

- 2 tbsp olive oil

- 2 tbsp chili powder

- 1 tsp cumin

- 1 tsp paprika

- 1 tsp garlic powder

- 1 tsp onion powder

- 1 tsp dried oregano

- 1 tsp salt

- 1 tsp black pepper

- Flour or corn tortillas, for serving

Instructions:

- In your large bowl, combine the chicken strips, red bell pepper, and yellow onion.

- In your small bowl, mix together the garlic, olive oil, chili powder, cumin, paprika, garlic powder, onion powder, dried oregano, salt, and black pepper.

- Pour the mixture over the chicken and vegetables in the large bowl, and toss until everything is evenly coated.

- Set the air fryer to 400°F.

- Place the chicken and vegetables in a single layer in the air fryer basket. Fry for 8-10 minutes, flipping halfway through until the chicken is cooked through and the vegetables are slightly charred.

- Serve the chicken fajitas in warm flour or corn tortillas.

Nutritional Information (per serving, using flour tortilla):

- Calories: 350

- Fat: 12g

- Saturated Fat: 3g

- Cholesterol: 72mg

- Sodium: 988mg

- Sugar: 5g

- Protein: 27g

- Carbohydrates: 36g - Fiber: 4g

6. AIR FRYER CHICKEN PARMESAN

Ingredients:

- 4 boneless, skinless chicken breasts

- 1 cup all-purpose flour

- 2 large eggs, beaten

- 1 cup Italian-seasoned breadcrumbs

- 1 cup grated Parmesan cheese

- 1 tsp garlic powder

- 1 tsp dried basil

- Salt and pepper to taste

- 1 cup marinara sauce

- One cup of shredded mozzarella cheese

Instructions:

- Set the air fryer to 400°F.

- In three separate shallow bowls, place the flour in the first, the beaten eggs in the second, and the breadcrumbs, Parmesan cheese, garlic powder, dried basil, salt, and pepper in the third.

- Coat each chicken breast in the flour, then dip in the beaten eggs, and finally coat with the breadcrumb mixture.

- Put the chicken breasts that have been covered with a coating in the air fryer basket making sure they are laid out in a single layer.

- Cook for 8 minutes, then flip the chicken and cook for an additional 8 minutes, or until the internal temperature reaches 165°F and the coating is crispy and golden brown.

- Remove the chicken from the air fryer and top each breast with marinara sauce and shredded mozzarella cheese.

- Cook the chicken for another 2-3 minutes in the air fryer, or until the cheddar is melted and bubbling.

Nutritional Information (per serving):

- Saturated Fat: 6g

- Fiber: 2g

- Cholesterol: 141mg

- Calories: 422

- Fat: 14g

- Sodium: 849mg

- Sugar: 4g   - Protein: 41g   - Carbohydrates: 31g

7. AIR FRYER CHICKEN WINGS

Ingredients:

- 2 lb. chicken wings
- 1 tsp. garlic powder
- 1 tsp. onion powder
- 1 tsp. paprika
- 1 tsp. dried basil
- 1 tsp. dried thyme
- Salt and pepper, to taste
- Cooking spray

Instructions:

- In a bowl, combine garlic powder, onion powder, paprika, basil, thyme, salt, and pepper.
- Place the chicken wings in the bowl and toss to coat with the seasoning mixture.
- Set your air fryer to 400°F.
- Spray the air fryer basket with cooking spray to grease it.
- Place the seasoned chicken wings in a single layer in the basket.
- Cook for 20-25 minutes, flipping the wings halfway through cooking.
- Once done, the skin should be crispy and the internal temperature should be 165°F.
- Serve the wings hot with your favorite dipping sauce.

Nutritional Information (per serving, based on 4 servings):

- Carbohydrates: 2 g
- Fiber: 1 g
- Sugar: 0 g
- Protein: 40 g
- Calories: 420
- Fat: 30 g
- Saturated Fat: 9 g
- Cholesterol: 165 mg
- Sodium: 600 mg

8. AIR FRYER FISH AND CHIPS

Ingredients:

- 4 (6 oz) cod fillets

- 1 cup all-purpose flour

- 1 tsp paprika

- 1 tsp garlic powder

- 1 tsp dried thyme

- 1 tsp dried basil

- Salt and pepper to taste

- 2 eggs, beaten

- 1 cup panko breadcrumbs

- 4 russet potatoes, sliced into wedges

- 2 tbsp olive oil

Instructions:

- In a large shallow dish, mix together the flour, paprika, garlic powder, thyme, basil, salt, and pepper.

- In a different shallow bowl, whisk the eggs.

- Now, in the third shallow dish, put the panko breadcrumbs.

- Coat each cod fillet in the flour mixture, then dip in the beaten eggs and finally coat in the panko breadcrumbs.

- In a bowl, mix the potato wedges with olive oil, salt, and pepper.

- Set your air fryer to 400°F.

- Place the coated cod fillets in the air fryer basket, making sure not to overcrowd them. Cook for 8-10 minutes or until the crust is golden and the fish is cooked through.

- Put the potato wedges in a different basket and bake them for 20-25 minutes until they are both crunchy and soft.

- Serve the air fryer fish and chips hot with your favorite dipping sauce.

Nutritional Information (per serving, based on 4 servings):

- Protein: 27 g

- Sodium: 800 mg

- Calories: 550

- Fat: 20 g

- Carbohydrates: 63 g

- Cholesterol: 170 mg

9. AIR FRYER FRIED CHICKEN

Ingredients:

- 4 boneless, skinless chicken breasts or thighs

- 1 cup buttermilk

- 1 tsp garlic powder

- 1 tsp paprika

- 1 tsp salt

- 1 tsp black pepper

- 1 cup all-purpose flour

- 1 tsp baking powder

- Vegetable oil spray

Instructions:

- In a large bowl, whisk together the buttermilk, garlic powder, paprika, salt, and black pepper.

- Add the chicken to the bowl and make sure it's fully coated in the marinade. Cover and refrigerate for at least 30 minutes or up to 8 hours.

- Now, Ii your separate bowl, mix together the flour and baking powder.

- Remove the chicken from the marinade and coat each piece in the flour mixture.

- Set the air fryer to 400°F.

- Lightly spray the basket of the air fryer with vegetable oil spray.

- Place the chicken in the basket, making sure they don't overlap.

- Cook the chicken for 12-15 minutes, or until the internal temperature reaches 165°F.

- Serve this dish warm and provide a sauce of your choice for dipping.

Nutritional Information (per serving): Serves 4

- Calories: 320

- Fat: 9g

- Carbohydrates: 28g

- Protein: 32g

- Sodium: 880mg

10. AIR FRYER MEATLOAF

Ingredients:

- 1.5 lbs. ground beef

- 1 cup breadcrumbs

- 1 large egg

- 1 small onion, finely chopped

- 3 cloves garlic, minced

- 1 tsp dried thyme

- 1 tsp dried basil

- 1 tsp dried oregano

- 1 tsp salt

- 1/2 tsp black pepper

- 1/2 cup ketchup

- 2 tbsp. brown sugar

- 2 tbsp. apple cider vinegar

- 1 tsp mustard

- 1 tsp Worcestershire sauce

Instructions:

● In a large mixing bowl, combine the ground beef, breadcrumbs, egg, onion, garlic, thyme, basil, oregano, salt, and pepper.

● In a separate bowl, whisk together the ketchup, brown sugar, apple cider vinegar, mustard, and Worcestershire sauce.

● Mix the sauce into the beef mixture.

● Grease the basket of your air fryer with cooking spray.

● Shape the beef mixture into a loaf and place it in the air fryer basket.

● Cook at 400°F for 25 minutes.

● Brush the meatloaf with additional sauce and cook for an additional 5 minutes.

● Let the meatloaf rest for 5 minutes before slicing and serving.

Nutritional Information (per serving, based on 8 servings):

- Carbohydrates: 18 g

- Protein: 26 g

- Sodium: 720 mg

- Cholesterol: 100 mg

- Fiber: 1 g

- Sugars: 13 g

- Calories: 330 - Fat: 17 g

11. AIR FRYER PORK CHOPS

Ingredients:

- 4 boneless pork chops, about 1 inch thick

- 1 teaspoon salt

- 1 teaspoon black pepper

- 1 teaspoon paprika

- 1 teaspoon garlic powder

- 1 teaspoon onion powder

- 1 teaspoon dried thyme

- 1 teaspoon dried rosemary

- 2 tablespoons olive oil

Instructions:

• In a small bowl, mix together the salt, pepper, paprika, garlic powder, onion powder, thyme, and rosemary.

• Rub the mixture on both sides of each pork chop.

• Set your air fryer to 400°F.

• Drizzle the olive oil over the pork chops and place them in a single layer in the air fryer basket.

• Cook the pork chops for 12-15 minutes or until they reach an internal temperature of 145°F.

• Cook the pork chops for an appropriate amount of time, flipping them halfway through. Once done, serve hot with your favorite side dishes.

Nutritional Information (per serving):

- Sodium: 779mg

- Carbohydrates: 1g

- Protein: 25g

- Fat: 18g

- Calories: 257

12. AIR FRYER PORK TENDERLOIN

Ingredients:

- 2 lbs pork tenderloin

- 2 tbsp olive oil

- 1 tsp salt

- 1 tsp black pepper

- 1 tsp garlic powder

- 1 tsp paprika

- 1 tsp dried thyme

- 1 tsp dried rosemary

Instructions:

- Preheat the air fryer to 400°F.

- In a small bowl, mix together olive oil, salt, pepper, garlic powder, paprika, thyme, and rosemary.

- Rub the pork tenderloin with the spice mixture, making sure to cover it evenly.

- Put the pork tenderloin into the air fryer basket.

- Cook for 20 minutes at 400°F, then use tongs to flip the pork over.

- Cook for an additional 15-20 minutes, or until the internal temperature of the pork reaches 145°F.

- Before slicing and serving the pork, let it rest for 5 minutes.

Nutritional Information (per serving, based on 8 servings):

- Fat: 11g

- Sodium: 390mg

- Calories: 240

- Carbohydrates: 1g

- Protein: 36g

13. AIR FRYER QUICHE

Ingredients:

- 1 refrigerated pie crust or homemade pie crust

- 4 large eggs

- 1 cup heavy cream

- 1 cup grated cheese (cheddar, Swiss, or any other variety)

- 1/2 cup diced ham

- 1/4 cup diced onion

- 1/4 cup diced bell pepper

- Salt and pepper, to taste

- Optional: herbs such as thyme or basil

Instructions:

- Preheat the air fryer to 350°F.

- Place the pie crust in a 9-inch quiche dish or pie dish.

- Now, get a medium bowl, and in your medium bowl, whisk together the eggs, heavy cream, and grated cheese.

- Stir in the ham, onion, bell pepper, salt, pepper, and any optional herbs.

- Pour the mixture into the pie crust.

- Place the dish in the air fryer and cook for 25-30 minutes or until the center is set and the top is golden brown.

- Remove from the air fryer and let it cool for 5 minutes before slicing and serving.

Nutritional Information (per slice, based on 8 slices):

- Fat: 22 g

- Saturated Fat: 12 g

- Protein: 14 g

- Cholesterol: 169 mg

- Sodium: 440 mg

- Carbohydrates: 11 g

- Fiber: 0 g

- Sugar: 2 g

- Calories: 285

14. AIR FRYER ROASTED TURKEY BREAST

Ingredients:

- 1 (4-5 lb) turkey breast

- 2 tbsp olive oil

- 1 tsp dried thyme

- 1 tsp dried rosemary

- 1 tsp garlic powder

- 1 tsp onion powder

- 1 tsp paprika

- 1 tsp salt

- 1 tsp black pepper

- 1/2 tsp cayenne pepper (this is optional)

Instructions:

- In a small bowl, mix together olive oil, thyme, rosemary, garlic powder, onion powder, paprika, salt, black pepper, and cayenne pepper (if using).

- Here you rinse the turkey breast and pat it dry. Rub the oil and spice mixture all over the turkey.

- Place the turkey breast in the air fryer basket, making sure it's not touching the sides or bottom of the basket.

- Set the air fryer temperature to 400°F and cook for 20-25 minutes per pound of turkey, or until the internal temperature reaches 165°F when checked with a meat thermometer.

- Once cooked, remove the turkey breast from the air fryer and let it rest for 5-10 minutes before carving.

Nutritional Information (Per Serving, based on 6 servings):

- Cholesterol: 135 mg

- Sodium: 714 mg

- Carbohydrates: 1 g

- Fiber: 0 g

- Sugar: 0 g

- Protein: 44 g

- Calories: 259

- Fat: 9 g

- Saturated Fat: 2 g

15. AIR FRYER SALMON WITH LEMON AND HERBS

Ingredients:

- 4 salmon fillets, skin removed

- Salt and pepper to taste

- 1 lemon, sliced

- 2 tablespoons olive oil

- 2 tablespoons fresh herbs (such as thyme, basil, or parsley), chopped

Instructions:

- Preheat the air fryer to 400°F.

- After which you season the salmon fillets with salt and pepper on both sides.

- Place the lemon slices in the bottom of the air fryer basket.

- You go again and place the salmon fillets on top of the lemon slices.

- Brush the salmon with olive oil and sprinkle with the chopped herbs.

- Air fry the salmon for 10-12 minutes, or until the internal temperature reaches 145°F.

- Serve the salmon with lemon wedges and extra herbs, if desired.

Nutritional Information (per serving): Serves 4

- Calories: 240

- Fat: 16 g

- Carbohydrates: 2 g

- Protein: 24 g

- Sodium: 140 mg

- Cholesterol: 65 mg

16. AIR FRYER SAUSAGE AND PEPPERS

Ingredients:

- 12 ounces of sausages, sliced

- 2 large green bell peppers, sliced

- 1 large onion, sliced

- 2 garlic cloves, minced

- 1 tablespoon olive oil

- Salt and pepper to taste

- Red pepper flakes to taste (optional)

- Two large red bell peppers, cut into slices

Instructions:

- Preheat your air fryer to 400°F.

- In a large bowl, mix together the sliced sausages, sliced bell peppers, sliced onion, minced garlic, olive oil, salt, pepper, and red pepper flakes (if using).

- Transfer the mixture to the air fryer basket and spread it out in an even layer.

- Cook for 15 to 20 minutes, stirring the mixture occasionally until the sausages are browned and the peppers are slightly charred.

- Serve the sausages and peppers hot with crusty bread or over pasta.

Nutritional Information (per serving)

- Cholesterol: 45mg

- Sodium: 558mg

- Carbohydrates: 8g

- Protein: 12g.

- Fiber: 2g

- Sugar: 4g

- Calories: 243

- Fat: 19g

- Saturated Fat: 6g

17. AIR FRYER SHRIMP SCAMPI

Ingredients:

- 1 lb large shrimp, peeled and deveined

- 4 tablespoons butter, melted

- 4 cloves garlic, minced

- 1/4 cup fresh lemon juice

- 2 tablespoons white wine (optional)

- Salt and pepper, to taste

- 1 tablespoon chopped fresh parsley and 1/2 teaspoon red pepper flakes

Instructions:

- Preheat the air fryer to 400°F.

- In a bowl, mix together melted butter, minced garlic, lemon juice, white wine (if using), salt, pepper, and red pepper flakes.

- Here you add the shrimp to the bowl and toss to coat evenly with the sauce.

- Transfer the shrimp to the air fryer basket, making sure they are spaced out evenly.

- Cook the shrimp for 8-10 minutes, or until they are pink and cooked through.

- Remove the shrimp from the air fryer and sprinkle with chopped parsley.

- Serve the shrimp scampi hot with some crusty bread or over a bed of pasta.

Nutritional Information (per serving, based on 4 servings):

- Saturated Fat: 8 g

- Protein: 23 g

- Cholesterol: 300 mg

- Sodium: 550 mg

- Carbohydrates: 3 g

- Calories: 210

- Fat: 14 g

18. AIR FRYER STUFFED BELL PEPPERS

Ingredients:

- 4 large bell peppers, any color

- 1 lb. ground beef or turkey

- 1 cup cooked rice

- 1 can (14.5 oz) diced tomatoes

- 1/2 cup chopped onion

- 1 tsp minced garlic

- 1 tsp dried basil

- 1 tsp dried oregano

- 1 tsp paprika

- Salt and pepper, to taste

- 1 cup shredded mozzarella cheese

- Non-stick cooking spray

Instructions:

- Preheat the air fryer to 400°F.

- To get started cut the tops off of the bell peppers and remove the seeds and membranes.

- In a large bowl, mix together the ground beef, cooked rice, diced tomatoes, onion, garlic, basil, oregano, paprika, salt, and pepper.

- Fill each bell pepper with the meat and rice mixture.

- Place the filled bell peppers in the air fryer basket and spray with non-stick cooking spray.

- Cook for 15 minutes.

- Remove the basket from the air fryer and sprinkle shredded mozzarella cheese on top of each pepper.

- Now, to round it all up, cook for an additional 5 minutes or until the cheese is melted.

Nutritional Information (per serving, based on 4 servings):

- Dietary Fiber: 3 g

- Sugar: 6 g

- Protein: 29 g

- Calories: 375

- Total Fat: 18 g

- Saturated Fat: 8 g

- Cholesterol: 85 mg - Sodium: 312 mg - Total Carbohydrates: 22 g

19. AIR FRYER TOFU AND VEGETABLE STIR FRY

Ingredients:

- 14 oz. extra-firm tofu drained and pressed
- 2 tbsp. cornstarch
- 1 tbsp. olive oil
- 1 red bell pepper, sliced
- 1 yellow onion, sliced
- 1 cup sliced mushrooms
- 2 garlic cloves, minced
- 1 cup snow peas
- 2 tbsp. low sodium soy sauce
- 1 tbsp. rice vinegar
- 1 tsp. cornstarch
- 2 tbsp. water

Instructions:

- Cut the tofu into 1-inch cubes and place them in a bowl. Mix the cornstarch in with the tofu and stir until the cubes are evenly covered.

- In a large air fryer basket, add the coated tofu cubes in a single layer. Set the temperature to 400°F and cook for 20 minutes, flipping the tofu cubes once halfway through.

- While the tofu is cooking, heat the olive oil in a large skillet over medium heat. Add the red bell pepper, yellow onion, mushrooms, and garlic, and cook until the vegetables are tender and slightly charred about 10 minutes.

- Add the snow peas to the skillet and cook for an additional 2 minutes.

- In a small bowl, whisk together the soy sauce, rice vinegar, cornstarch, and water. Add the mixture to the skillet and stir until the sauce thickens about 2 minutes.

- Add the cooked tofu cubes to the skillet and gently toss to evenly coat the tofu with the sauce.

- Serve the stir fry hot over rice or noodles.

Nutritional Information (Per Serving): Servings: 4- Carbohydrates: 11g - Protein: 14g

- Sodium: 474mg

- Calories: 214

- Fat: 14g

20. AIR FRYER VEGGIE BURGERS

Ingredients:

- 1 can black beans, drained and rinsed
- 1 cup diced mushrooms
- 1/2 cup grated carrots
- 1/2 cup diced onion
- 1/2 cup breadcrumbs
- 2 tablespoons finely chopped fresh cilantro
- 1 tablespoon olive oil
- 1 teaspoon chili powder
- 1 teaspoon cumin
- Salt and pepper, to taste
- Two Tbsp of finely chopped parsley, fresh
- One cup of cooked brown rice
- 4 whole wheat buns
- Toppings of your choice (lettuce, tomato, avocado, cheese, etc.)

Instructions:

- In a large mixing bowl, combine the cooked brown rice, black beans, mushrooms, carrots, and onion.
- In a separate small mixing bowl, mix together the breadcrumbs, parsley, cilantro, olive oil, chili powder, cumin, salt, and pepper.
- Add the breadcrumb mixture to the large bowl with the rice and veggies and mix well until everything is evenly combined.
- Divide the mixture into 4 equal portions and form each into a patty.
- Place the patties in the air fryer basket and cook at 400°F for 15-18 minutes, flipping halfway through, until the outside is crispy and the inside is heated through.
- Toast the whole wheat buns in the air fryer for a minute or two.
- Serve the veggie burgers on the toasted buns with your choice of toppings.

Nutritional Information (per serving, with a whole wheat bun): - Cholesterol: 0mg - Sodium: 655mg

- Carbohydrates: 66g - Fiber: 10g - Sugar: 7g
- Protein: 13g
- Calories: 425
- Fat: 12g   - Saturated Fat: 2

21. AIR FRYER BUFFALO CAULIFLOWER BITES

Ingredients:

- 1 large head of cauliflower, cut into bite-sized florets

- 1 cup all-purpose flour

- 1 tsp garlic powder

- 1 tsp onion powder

- 1 tsp paprika

- 1/2 tsp cayenne pepper

- 1 tsp salt

- 1 tsp black pepper

- 1 cup almond milk

- 1 cup panko breadcrumbs

- 1/2 cup hot sauce

- Two tbsp unsalted butter, melted

Instructions:

- In a mixing bowl, whisk together the flour, garlic powder, onion powder, paprika, cayenne pepper, salt, and black pepper.

- In a separate bowl, pour in the almond milk.

- Get a third bowl and in your third bowl, pour in the panko breadcrumbs.

- Dip each cauliflower floret in the flour mixture, then into the almond milk, and finally into the panko breadcrumbs.

- Repeat this process for all the cauliflower florets and set them aside on a plate.

- Preheat your air fryer to 400°F for 5 minutes.

- Once preheated, place the coated cauliflower florets into the air fryer basket in a single layer.

- Cook for 15 minutes, flipping the florets over halfway through.

- In your mixing bowl, whisk together the hot sauce and melted butter.

- Once the cauliflower is done cooking, remove it from the air fryer and place it in the bowl with the hot sauce mixture. Toss until the florets are evenly coated.

- Return the coated cauliflower back to the air fryer and cook for an additional 5 minutes.

- Enjoy the dish right away accompanied by your preferred dipping sauce.

Nutritional Information (per serving, based on 8 servings):

- Cholesterol: 10mg

- Sodium: 1036mg

- Carbohydrates: 17.5g

- Fiber: 2.5g

- Sugar: 4.8g

- Protein: 6.5g

- Calories: 146

- Fat: 6.2g

- Saturated Fat: 2.3g

22. AIR FRYER GRILLED CHEESE SANDWICH

Ingredients:

- 2 slices of cheese (cheddar, mozzarella, or any cheese of your choice)

- 1 tablespoon butter, melted

- Salt and pepper, to taste

- Two slices of bread

Instructions:

- Set your air fryer to 400°F (200°C).

- Take two slices of bread and place a slice of cheese between them.

- Brush the melted butter on the outside of the sandwich.

- Add salt and pepper to taste.

- Place the sandwich in the air fryer basket, making sure it is evenly spaced.

- Cook the sandwich for 4-5 minutes or until the cheese is melted and the bread is golden brown.

- Remove the sandwich from the air fryer and let it cool for a minute or two.

- Serve and enjoy your delicious air fryer grilled cheese sandwich!

Nutritional Information (per serving):

- Calories: 256

- Fat: 17g

- Sodium: 654mg

- Carbohydrates: 14g

- Protein: 13g

23. AIR FRYER STEAK

Ingredients:

- 2 (6-8 oz) sirloin steaks, at room temperature

- 1 tbsp olive oil

- 1 tsp garlic powder

- 1 tsp dried thyme

- 1 tsp paprika

- Salt and pepper, to taste

Instructions:

- Preheat the air fryer to 400°F.

- In a small bowl, mix together the olive oil, garlic powder, thyme, paprika, salt, and pepper.

- Rub the steaks with the mixture, making sure to coat them evenly.

- Place the steaks in the air fryer basket and cook for 6-8 minutes, flipping them once halfway through cooking.

- Check the internal temperature of the steaks using a meat thermometer. For medium-rare, the temperature should reach 145°F. For medium, the temperature should reach 160°F.

- Remove the steaks from the air fryer and let them rest for 5 minutes before slicing and serving.

Nutritional Information (per serving, based on 2 steaks):

- Saturated Fat: 11g

- Protein: 36g

- Cholesterol: 116mg

- Sodium: 149mg

- Total Carbohydrates: 2g

- Calories: 405

- Total Fat: 30g

24. AIR FRYER SWEET POTATO FRIES

Ingredients:

- 2 large sweet potatoes

- 2 tbsp olive oil

- 1 tsp salt

- 1 tsp black pepper

- 1 tsp paprika

- 1 tsp garlic powder

Instructions:

- Wash and peel the sweet potatoes, then cut them into thin fry-shaped slices.

- In a large bowl, mix together the sliced sweet potatoes, olive oil, salt, pepper, paprika, and garlic powder. Toss until the sweet potatoes are evenly coated.

- Preheat your air fryer to 400°F for about 3-5 minutes.

- Place the sweet potato slices in a single layer in the basket of your air fryer, leaving some space between each slice.

- Cook the sweet potato fries for 15-20 minutes, flipping them once or twice during cooking until they are golden brown and crispy.

- Remove the sweet potato fries from the air fryer and place them on a paper towel-lined plate to absorb any excess oil.

- Serve hot with your favorite dipping sauce, such as ketchup, ranch, or honey mustard.

Nutritional Information (per serving, about 1/4 of the recipe):

- Carbohydrates: 22 g

- Protein: 2 g

- Sodium: 550 mg

- Calories: 150

- Fat: 7 g

- Fiber: 3 g

25. AIR FRYER ZUCCHINI FRITTERS

Ingredients:

- 2 medium zucchinis, grated

- 1/4 cup all-purpose flour

- 1 egg

- 1/4 cup parmesan cheese, grated

- 1/4 teaspoon salt

- 1/4 teaspoon black pepper

- 1/4 teaspoon garlic powder

- 1/4 teaspoon onion powder

- 1/4 teaspoon paprika

- Non-stick cooking spray

Instructions:

- Starting with setting your air fryer to 400°F (200°C).

- In a large mixing bowl, combine the grated zucchini, flour, egg, parmesan cheese, salt, black pepper, garlic powder, onion powder, and paprika.

- Mix the ingredients together until well combined.

- Apply a thin layer of non-stick cooking spray to the air fryer basket. Using a spoon or cookie scoop, form the mixture into 2-3 inch fritters.

- Place the fritters into the air fryer basket, making sure they are not touching.

- Cook for 5 minutes, then flip and cook for an additional 5 minutes.

- Once the fritters are crispy and golden brown, remove them from the air fryer and place them on a paper towel-lined plate to remove any excess oil.

- Enjoy your favorite dipping sauce with this.

Nutritional Information: Servings: 4 Serving size: 2 fritters. Amount per serving:

- Dietary Fiber: 1g

- Sugar: 2g

- Calories: 99

- Total Fat: 5g

- Saturated Fat: 2g

- Cholesterol: 56mg

- Sodium: 363mg

- Total Carbohydrates: 9g - Protein: 6g

PART THREE

APPETIZERS AND SNACKS

1. AIR FRYER AVOCADO FRIES

Ingredients:

- 2 ripe avocados

- 1 cup panko breadcrumbs

- 1/2 cup all-purpose flour

- 2 eggs, beaten

- 1 tsp garlic powder

- 1 tsp paprika

- Salt and pepper to taste

Instructions:

• Cut the avocados in half, remove the pit, and slice each half into 4 slices.

• In a shallow dish, mix together the panko breadcrumbs, garlic powder, paprika, salt, and pepper.

• Place the flour in a separate shallow bowl.

• In a third shallow dish, beat the eggs.

• Dip each avocado slice in the flour, shaking off any excess, then dip it into the beaten eggs, making sure it's evenly coated.

• Finally, coat each slice in the breadcrumb mixture, making sure it's fully coated.

• Preheat the air fryer to 400°F for 3-5 minutes.

• Place the breaded avocado slices in a single layer in the air fryer basket, making sure not to overcrowd it.

• Cook for 8-10 minutes or until golden brown, flipping the slices halfway through.

• Serve the avocado fries hot with your favorite dipping sauce, if that's how you like it.

Nutritional Information (per serving, based on 8 slices per avocado):

- Carbohydrates: 16g

- Fiber: 7g

- Sugar: 1g

- Sodium: 290mg

- Calories: 245

- Fat: 20g

- Protein: 5g

2. AIR FRYER BACON-WRAPPED JALAPENOS

Ingredients:

- 8 jalapeno peppers, sliced in half lengthwise and seeds removed

- 8 ounces of cream cheese, brought to room temperature

- 1 cup shredded cheddar cheese

- 8 slices of bacon, cut in half

Instructions:

- Set your air fryer to 400°F (200°C) for about 5 minutes.

- In a bowl, mix together the cream cheese and shredded cheddar cheese.

- Fill each jalapeno half with the cheese mixture, using a spoon or small spatula.

- Wrap each jalapeno half with half a slice of bacon, securing it with a toothpick.

- Place the wrapped jalapenos in the air fryer basket in a single layer, making sure they are not touching.

- Cook in the air fryer for 8-10 minutes, or until the bacon is crispy and the cheese is melted and bubbly.

- Serve the bacon-wrapped jalapenos hot, garnished with chopped fresh parsley or cilantro if desired.

Nutritional Information (per serving, 4 pieces):

- Sodium: 550 mg

- Calories: 300

- Total Fat: 26 g

- Saturated Fat: 12 g

- Protein: 13 g.

- Cholesterol: 60 mg

- Total Carbohydrates: 7 g

- Dietary Fiber: 1 g

- Sugar: 3 g

3. CRISPY AIR FRYER CHICKPEAS

Ingredients:

- 1 can of chickpeas (15 ounces)

- 1 teaspoon of olive oil

- Half a teaspoon of garlic powder

- 1 smoked paprika teaspoon

- A quarter teaspoon of cumin

- Add black pepper and salt to taste.

Instructions:

- Set the air fryer to 400 degrees Fahrenheit (200 degrees Celsius).

- After draining and rinsing the chickpeas, wipe them dry with paper towels.

- Combine the chickpeas, olive oil, garlic powder, smoked paprika, cumin, salt, and black pepper in a mixing bowl.

- Cook for 12-15 minutes, shaking the basket halfway through, with the seasoned chickpeas in the air fryer basket.

- Remove the chickpeas from the air fryer when they are golden brown and crispy, and serve immediately.

Nutritional Information (per serving, based on 4 servings):

- Calories: 98

- Fat: 3g

- Saturated Fat: 0g

- Cholesterol: 0mg

- Sodium: 176mg

- Carbohydrates: 13g

- Fiber: 3g

- Sugars: 1g

- Protein: 4g

4. AIR FRYER CHEESY GARLIC BREAD

Ingredients:

- 4 slices of white bread

- 4 tbsp butter, softened

- 2 cloves of garlic, minced

- 1/2 cup shredded mozzarella cheese

- Salt and pepper, to taste

- Two tbsp fresh parsley, chopped

Instructions:

- Preheat your air fryer to 400°F.

- In a small mixing bowl, mix together the softened butter, minced garlic, chopped parsley, salt, and pepper until well combined.

- So, what you will do here is spread the butter equally on each piece of bread.

- Sprinkle the shredded mozzarella cheese on top of the bread slices.

- Place the slices of bread in the air fryer basket in a single layer, making sure they don't overlap.

- Cook in the air fryer for 5-7 minutes or until the cheese is melted and the bread is toasted to your liking.

- Serve hot and enjoy your delicious, cheesy garlic bread!

Nutritional Information (per slice):

- Cholesterol: 40mg

- Sodium: 400mg

- Carbohydrates: 18g

- Calories: 240

- Fiber: 1g

- Sugar: 1g

- Protein: 7g

- Fat: 16g

- Saturated Fat: 9g

5. AIR FRYER EGG ROLLS

Ingredients:

- 8 wrappers for egg rolls

- 1 cup diced and cooked veggies (such as carrots, cabbage, and onions)

- 1 cup drained and cooked noodles

- 2 tbsp of soy sauce

- 1 teaspoon hoisin sauce

- 1 tbsp sesame oil

- 1 tsp cornstarch

- 1 beaten egg

- One cup of shredded cooked chicken

Instructions:

- Combine the chicken, veggies, noodles, soy sauce, hoisin sauce, sesame oil, and cornstarch in a large mixing bowl.

- Place an egg roll wrapper on a flat surface and fill it with 2 teaspoons of the mixture.

- Roll the wrapper around the filling securely, folding in the sides as you go. Seal the edges with the beaten egg.

- Repeat the technique with the remaining wrappers and filling.

- Carefully place the egg rolls in the air fryer basket in a single layer.

- Preheat the air fryer to 375°F and cook the egg rolls for 8-10 minutes, or until golden brown and crispy.

- Serve right away with your favorite dipping sauce.

Nutritional Information (per serving, based on 8 servings):

- Fat: 6g

- Saturated Fat: 2g

- Cholesterol: 57mg

- Sodium: 574mg

- Calories: 180

- Carbohydrates: 22g

- Fiber: 1g

- Protein: 10g

- Sugar: 2g

6. AIR FRYER FALAFEL

Ingredients:

- 1 can (15 oz) chickpeas, drained and rinsed

- 1/2 cup finely chopped onion

- 3 cloves garlic, minced

- 1/4 cup parsley, chopped

- 1/4 cup cilantro, chopped

- 2 tablespoons flour

- 1 teaspoon ground cumin

- 1 teaspoon ground coriander

- 1/2 teaspoon baking powder

- Salt and pepper, to taste

- Oil, for brushing

Instructions:

- In a food processor, pulse the chickpeas, onion, garlic, parsley, and cilantro until roughly chopped.

- Add the flour, cumin, coriander, baking powder, salt, and pepper to the chickpea mixture and pulse until combined and a sticky dough forms.

- Roll the dough into a 1 1/2-inch ball and press to flatten slightly.

- Apply a thin layer of oil to the falafel.

- Place the falafel in the air fryer basket in a single layer, making sure not to overcrowd the basket.

- Cook the falafel at 400°F for 8-10 minutes, flipping once, until golden brown and crispy.

- Serve the falafel hot, topped with your favorite sauce, or in a pita with veggies and tahini sauce.

Nutritional Information (per serving, based on 12 falafel):

- Saturated Fat: 1g

- Carbohydrates: 18g

- Fiber: 4g

- Protein: 5g

- Sodium: 150mg

- Calories: 120

- Fat: 4g

7. AIR FRYER FRENCH TOAST STICKS

Ingredients:

- 6 slices of bread (stale bread works best)

- 2 large eggs

- 1/2 cup of milk

- 1 tsp of vanilla extract

- 1/4 tsp of cinnamon

- 2 tbsp of sugar

- 1 tsp of unsalted butter

- Cooking spray

Instructions:

- To get started cut each slice of bread into 4 sticks.

- In a large mixing bowl, whisk together the eggs, milk, vanilla extract, cinnamon, and sugar.

- Dip each stick of bread into the egg mixture, making sure to coat both sides.

- In your small saucepan, melt the butter. Using a pastry brush, brush the melted butter onto the bottom and sides of the air fryer basket.

- Place the coated bread sticks in a single layer in the air fryer basket.

- Lightly spray the top of the breadsticks with cooking spray.

- Air fry the French toast sticks at 375°F for 8-10 minutes, flipping once halfway through until they are golden brown.

- Serve the French toast sticks hot with your favorite syrup and toppings, such as fresh fruit, whipped cream, and powdered sugar.

Nutritional Information: Serves 6 Per serving (based on 2 sticks per serving):

- Sugar: 13 g

- Protein: 8 g.

- Calories: 200

- Fat: 7 g

- Saturated Fat: 3 g

- Cholesterol: 106 mg

- Sodium: 240 mg

- Carbohydrates: 27 g

- Fiber: 1 g

8. AIR FRYER FRIED PICKLES

Ingredients:

- 16 oz jar of dill pickle slices
- 1 cup all-purpose flour
- 2 teaspoons paprika
- 1 teaspoon garlic powder
- 1 teaspoon onion powder
- 1 teaspoon dried oregano
- 1 teaspoon dried basil
- 1/2 teaspoon dried thyme
- 1/2 teaspoon cayenne pepper
- 1 teaspoon salt
- 1/2 teaspoon black pepper
- 2 large eggs
- 1/4 cup milk
- 1 1/2 cups panko bread crumbs

Instructions:

- Drain the pickle slices and pat them dry with paper towels.
- In a medium-sized bowl, whisk together the flour, paprika, garlic powder, onion powder, oregano, basil, thyme, cayenne pepper, salt, and black pepper.
- In another bowl, whisk together the eggs and milk.
- Place the panko bread crumbs in a third bowl.
- Dip each pickle slice into the flour mixture, then the egg mixture, and finally the panko bread crumbs, making sure to coat each slice evenly.
- Place the coated pickle slices in a single layer in the air fryer basket.
- Set the air fryer to 400°F and cook for 8-10 minutes, or until the pickles are golden brown and crispy.

Nutritional Information (per serving, based on 8 servings): - Saturated Fat: 2 g - Calories: 198 - Fat: 11 g - Cholesterol: 55 mg

- Sodium: 982 mg
- Fiber: 1 g
- Sugar: 2 g
- Protein: 6 g
- Carbohydrates: 19 g

9. AIR FRYER CRAB RANGOON

Ingredients:

- 1 tsp mayonnaise

- 1/4 teaspoon garlic powder

- 1 6-ounce can of crabmeat, drained and flaked

- 1 /4 teaspoon Worcestershire sauce

- 1/4 teaspoon paprika

- 24 wonton wrappers

- 2 tablespoons butter, melted

- Two tablespoons finely chopped onion

- One eight-ounce package of cream cheese softened

Instructions:

- Set the oven to 350 degrees F.

- In your medium bowl, combine cream cheese, crabmeat, onion, mayonnaise, garlic powder, Worcestershire sauce, and paprika. Mix well.

- Put a wonton wrapper on a clean surface. Place 1 tablespoon of the cream cheese mixture in the center of the wrapper.

- Moisten the edges of the wrapper with water and fold it in half to form a triangle. Press edges together to seal.

- Place the crab rangoons on a baking sheet lined with parchment paper. Brush the tops of the rangoons with melted butter.

- Place the dish in the oven and bake for 15 minutes, or until the surface is golden brown.

- Once done, remove from the oven and serve warm with your preferred dipping sauce.

Nutritional Information: Serving size: 1 crab Rangoon - Sodium: 150mg

- Carbohydrates: 4.7g

- Fiber: 0g

- Sugar: 0.4g

- Protein: 3.2g

- Fat: 5.4g

- Saturated fat: 3.2g

- Calories: 80

- Trans-fat: 0g   - Cholesterol: 15mg

10. AIR FRYER MOZZARELLA STICKS

Ingredients:

- 1 cup Italian-seasoned breadcrumbs

- 2 eggs, beaten

- 2 tablespoons all-purpose flour

- Salt and pepper, to taste

- Eight frozen mozzarella sticks

Instructions:

• Set the air fryer to 400°F.

• In a shallow dish, mix the breadcrumbs, salt, and pepper.

• In your separate shallow dish, beat the eggs.

• Now get a shallow bowl and in your shallow bowl, place the flour separately.

• Dredge each mozzarella stick in the flour, then in the beaten eggs, and finally in the breadcrumb mixture, making sure each stick is fully coated.

• Place the coated mozzarella sticks in the air fryer basket in a single layer, making sure there is space between each stick.

• Cook the mozzarella sticks for 8-10 minutes, or until they are golden brown and crispy. Flip the sticks once during cooking.

• Serve the mozzarella sticks with your favorite dipping sauce, such as marinara, ranch, or garlic aioli.

Nutritional Information (per serving, 2 mozzarella sticks)

- Sugar: 2g

- Calories: 250

- Fat: 16g

- Saturated Fat: 8g

- Cholesterol: 70mg

- Sodium: 550mg

- Carbohydrates: 18g

- Fiber: 1g

- Protein: 11g

11. AIR FRYER ONION RINGS

Ingredients:

- 1 large onion, sliced into rings

- 1 cup all-purpose flour

- 1 teaspoon paprika

- 1 teaspoon garlic powder

- 1 teaspoon salt

- 1/2 teaspoon black pepper

- 1 cup buttermilk

- 1 egg

- 2 cups breadcrumbs

- Cooking spray

Instructions:

- Preheat the air fryer to 400°F.

- In a shallow dish, mix together the flour, paprika, garlic powder, salt, and black pepper.

- In a separate shallow dish, beat the egg and mix in the buttermilk.

- In your third shallow dish, place the breadcrumbs.

- Dip each onion ring into the flour mixture, shaking off any excess.

- Then dip the onion ring into the buttermilk mixture, making sure it's well coated.

- Finally, roll the onion ring in the breadcrumbs, making sure it's well coated.

- Repeat the process with all the onion rings.

- Lightly spray the air fryer basket with cooking spray.

- Place the coated onion rings in the air fryer basket in a single layer, making sure they don't overlap.

- Cook for 10 minutes, flipping the onion rings halfway through.

- Once the onion rings are golden brown and crispy, remove them from the air fryer and serve immediately with your favorite dipping sauce.

Nutritional Information per serving (based on 8 servings): - Cholesterol: 40mg - Sodium: 614mg - Carbohydrates: 24.7g - Fiber: 1.7g - Sugar: 3.2g

- Protein: 7.3g   - Calories: 208   - Fat: 8.4g
- Saturated Fat: 1.7g

12. AIR FRYER PARMESAN ZUCCHINI COINS

Ingredients:

- 2 medium zucchinis, sliced into 1/4 inch rounds

- 1/2 cup all-purpose flour

- 2 eggs, beaten

- 1 cup panko breadcrumbs

- 1/2 cup grated parmesan cheese

- Salt and pepper, to taste

- Cooking spray

Instructions:

- Preheat the air fryer to 400°F.

- In a shallow dish, the flour should be added.

- In another shallow dish, the beaten eggs should be added.

- In your third shallow dish, combine the panko breadcrumbs, parmesan cheese, salt, and pepper.

- Dip each zucchini round into the flour, then the egg mixture, and finally into the panko mixture, making sure to coat it evenly.

- Spray the air fryer basket with a light coating of cooking spray.

- Place the coated zucchini rounds into the air fryer basket in a single layer, making sure to not overcrowd the basket.

- Cook for 8-10 minutes or until golden brown and crispy.

- Enjoy the dish warm with a sauce of your preference.

Nutritional Information (Per serving, based on 4 servings):

- Fiber: 2g

- Fat: 8g

- Saturated Fat: 3g

- Cholesterol: 93mg

- Sodium: 314mg

- Calories: 174

- Carbohydrates: 18g

- Sugar: 3g

- Protein: 8g

13. AIR FRYER PIZZA ROLLS

Ingredients:

- 8 frozen pizza rolls

- Non-stick cooking spray

- 2 teaspoons Italian seasoning

- 1/4 teaspoon garlic powder

- Salt and pepper to taste

- 1 tablespoon grated parmesan cheese (optional)

Instructions:

- Preheat the air fryer to 400°F.

- Remove the frozen pizza rolls from their packaging and place them in a single layer in the air fryer basket.

- Spray the pizza rolls with a light coat of non-stick cooking spray.

- In a small bowl, mix together the Italian seasoning, garlic powder, salt, and pepper. Sprinkle the mixture over the pizza rolls.

- If desired, sprinkle parmesan cheese over the top of the pizza rolls.

- Place the basket into the preheated air fryer and cook for 10-12 minutes, or until the pizza rolls are crispy and golden brown on the outside.

- Remove the pizza rolls from the air fryer and serve immediately, while they are still hot.

Nutritional Information (per serving, based on 8 pizza rolls):

- Calories: 220

- Fat: 12g

- Saturated Fat: 4g

- Cholesterol: 20mg

- Sodium: 420mg

- Carbohydrates: 22g

- Fiber: 1g

- Sugar: 3g

- Protein: 7g

14. AIR FRYER PANKO CRUSTED SHRIMP

Ingredients:

- 1 lb raw shrimp, peeled and deveined

- 1 cup panko breadcrumbs

- 1/2 cup all-purpose flour

- 2 eggs, beaten

- 1 tsp garlic powder

- 1 tsp onion powder

- 1 tsp paprika

- 1/2 tsp salt

- 1/4 tsp black pepper

- Cooking spray

- Lemon wedges for serving (optional)

Instructions:

- Preheat the air fryer to 400°F.

- In a shallow dish, mix together the panko breadcrumbs, garlic powder, onion powder, paprika, salt, and black pepper.

- In your third shallow dish, place the beaten eggs.

- In a separate shallow dish, place the flour.

- Dredge each shrimp first in the flour, then in the eggs, and finally in the panko mixture, making sure they are evenly coated with each.

- Lightly spray the air fryer basket with cooking spray.

- Place the coated shrimp in a single layer in the air fryer basket, making sure not to overcrowd the basket.

- Air fry for 8-10 minutes or until the shrimp is golden brown and crispy.

- You can choose to serve it with lemon wedges if desired.

Nutritional Information (per serving, based on 4 servings):

- Calories: 320

- Protein: 27g

- Fat: 10g

- Carbohydrates: 29g

- Sodium: 940mg

- Fiber: 2g

- Sugar: 2g

15. AIR FRYER PORK RINDS

Ingredients:

- 1 (8 oz) bag of pork rinds

- 1 tsp. salt

- 1 tsp. black pepper

- 1 tsp. garlic powder

- 1 tsp. onion powder

- 1 tsp. paprika

Instructions:

- Preheat your air fryer to 400°F.

- In a large bowl, combine the pork rinds with the salt, black pepper, garlic powder, onion powder, and paprika.

- Place the seasoned pork rinds in a single layer in the air fryer basket.

- Cook for 7-8 minutes or until crispy and golden brown, shaking the basket halfway through cooking.

- Remove the pork rinds from the air fryer and place them on a paper towel-lined plate to drain any excess grease.

- Serve hot and enjoy.

Nutritional Information (per serving): Serves 4 Amount per serving:

- Cholesterol: 30mg

- Sodium: 450mg

- Total Carbohydrates: 0g

- Dietary Fiber: 0g

- Sugars: 0g

- Protein: 12g

- Calories: 160

- Total Fat: 12g

- Saturated Fat: 4g

16. AIR FRYER SWEET POTATO FRIES

Ingredients:

- 2 medium sweet potatoes, peeled and sliced into 1/4-inch sticks

- 2 tbsp olive oil

- 1 tsp salt

- 1 tsp black pepper

- 1 tsp paprika

- 1 tsp garlic powder

- 1 tsp dried thyme

Instructions:

- Set the air fryer to 400°F (200°C).

- In a large bowl, toss together the sweet potato sticks, olive oil, salt, pepper, paprika, garlic powder, and thyme until the sweet potatoes are evenly coated.

- Place the sweet potato sticks in a single layer in the basket of the air fryer.

- Cook for 10-15 minutes, flipping the sweet potatoes halfway through until they are golden brown and crispy.

- Serve immediately, with your favorite dipping sauce, if desired.

Nutritional Information (per serving, based on 4 servings):

- Cholesterol: 0mg

- Protein: 2g

- Sodium: 638mg

- Carbohydrates: 26g

- Calories: 218

- Fat: 12g

- Saturated Fat: 2g

- Fiber: 4g

- Sugar: 5g

17. AIR FRYER TOASTED RAVIOLI

Ingredients:

- 18-20 frozen cheese ravioli

- 1/2 cup all-purpose flour

- 2 large eggs, beaten

- 1 cup panko bread crumbs

- Salt and pepper, to taste

- Olive oil cooking spray

Instructions:

- Preheat the air fryer to 400°F.

- In a shallow dish, place the flour.

- In another shallow dish, beat the eggs with a fork.

- In a third shallow dish, mix the panko bread crumbs with salt and pepper.

- Dip each ravioli in the flour, then into the beaten eggs, and finally into the panko mixture, making sure each side is well coated.

- Place the coated ravioli in the air fryer basket in a single layer, leaving some space between each one.

- Give the ravioli a light coating of olive oil cooking spray.

- Cook for 8-10 minutes, or until the panko coating is golden brown and crispy.

- Serve hot with your favorite marinara sauce.

Nutritional Information (per serving, based on 20 ravioli):

- Saturated Fat: 2g

- Cholesterol: 80mg

- Calories: 140

- Total Fat: 5g

- Sodium: 220mg

- Total Carbohydrates: 16g

- Dietary Fiber: 1g

- Sugars: 1g

- Protein: 6g

18. AIR FRYER VEGETABLE SPRING ROLLS

Ingredients:

- 8 spring roll wrappers
- 1 cup shredded carrots
- 1 cup shredded cabbage
- 1 cup sliced mushrooms
- 1/2 cup diced onion
- 2 cloves garlic, minced
- 1 cup cooked brown rice
- 2 tablespoons soy sauce
- 2 tablespoons hoisin sauce
- 1 teaspoon sesame oil
- 1 tablespoon cornstarch
- 1 tablespoon water
- Oil for brushing the spring rolls

Instructions:

- In a large skillet, heat a small amount of oil over medium heat.
- Add the onions and garlic and cook until softened, about 2-3 minutes.
- Add the mushrooms, cabbage, and carrots and cook until tender, about 5-7 minutes.
- Add the cooked brown rice, soy sauce, hoisin sauce, and sesame oil to the pan and stir to combine.
- In your small bowl, mix together the cornstarch and water to make a slurry.
- Pour the slurry into the pan with the vegetables and stir to combine.
- Cook until the mixture has thickened, about 2-3 minutes.
- Set your air fryer to 400°F (200°C).
- Lay a spring roll wrapper on a clean surface and place about 2 tablespoons of the vegetable mixture in the center of the wrapper.
- Roll the wrapper tightly, sealing the edges, and brush with a small amount of oil.
- Use the leftover spring roll wrappers and filling to repeat the process.
- Place the spring rolls in the air fryer basket, making sure they are not touching.

- Cook for 8-10 minutes, flipping the spring rolls halfway through cooking until they are golden brown and crispy.

- Serve immediately with your chosen dipping sauce.

Nutritional Information (per serving, 2 spring rolls):

- Cholesterol: 0mg

- Sodium: 800mg

- Carbohydrates: 38g

- Fiber: 2g

- Sugar: 6g

- Protein: 6g

- Calories: 230

- Fat: 7g

- Saturated Fat: 1g

19. AIR-FRIED COCONUT SHRIMP

Ingredients:

- 1 lb. large raw shrimp, peeled and deveined
- 1/2 cup all-purpose flour
- 2 eggs, lightly beaten
- 1 cup unsweetened coconut flakes
- 1 teaspoon garlic powder
- 1 teaspoon paprika
- 1/2 teaspoon salt
- 1/4 teaspoon black pepper
- Oil for air-frying

Instructions:

- Preheat the air-fryer to 375 degrees F.
- In a shallow bowl, combine flour, garlic powder, paprika, salt, and pepper.
- Get another shallow bowl and in that shallow bowl, whisk the eggs.
- Place coconut flakes in a third shallow bowl.
- Working one at a time, dip each shrimp first in the flour, then the eggs, and lastly in the coconut flakes.
- Put the shrimp that has been covered in the air-fryer basket.
- Cook for 8 minutes, flipping the shrimp halfway through.
- Serve immediately.

Nutritional Information (per serving):

- Calories: 213
- Fat: 9.5 g
- Carbohydrates: 13.5 g
- Protein: 21.5 g
- Sodium: 545 mg
- Fiber: 3 g

20. AIR FRYER BUFFALO CHICKEN DIP

Ingredients:

- 2 boneless skinless chicken breasts, cooked and shredded

- 8 oz cream cheese, softened

- 1/2 cup hot sauce

- 1/2 cup shredded cheddar cheese

- 1/4 cup diced celery

- Two tbsp chopped green onions

- 1/2 cup blue cheese or ranch dressing

- Salt and pepper, to taste

Instructions:

- Preheat the air fryer to 400°F.

- In your large bowl, mix together the shredded chicken, cream cheese, hot sauce, blue cheese or ranch dressing, shredded cheddar cheese, diced celery, green onions, salt, and pepper.

- Spoon the mixture into a greased 8-inch square baking dish.

- Place the dish in the air fryer basket and cook for 10-12 minutes, or until the cheese is melted and the dip is heated through.

- Serve hot with crackers, vegetables, or tortilla chips.

4 Servings (Nutritional Information) Serving size: 1/4 of the recipe:

- Dietary Fiber: 0 g

- Sugars: 3 g

- Protein: 19 g

- Calories: 445

- Fat: 42 g

- Saturated Fat: 20 g

- Cholesterol: 123 mg

- Sodium: 1097 mg

- Total Carbohydrates: 8 g

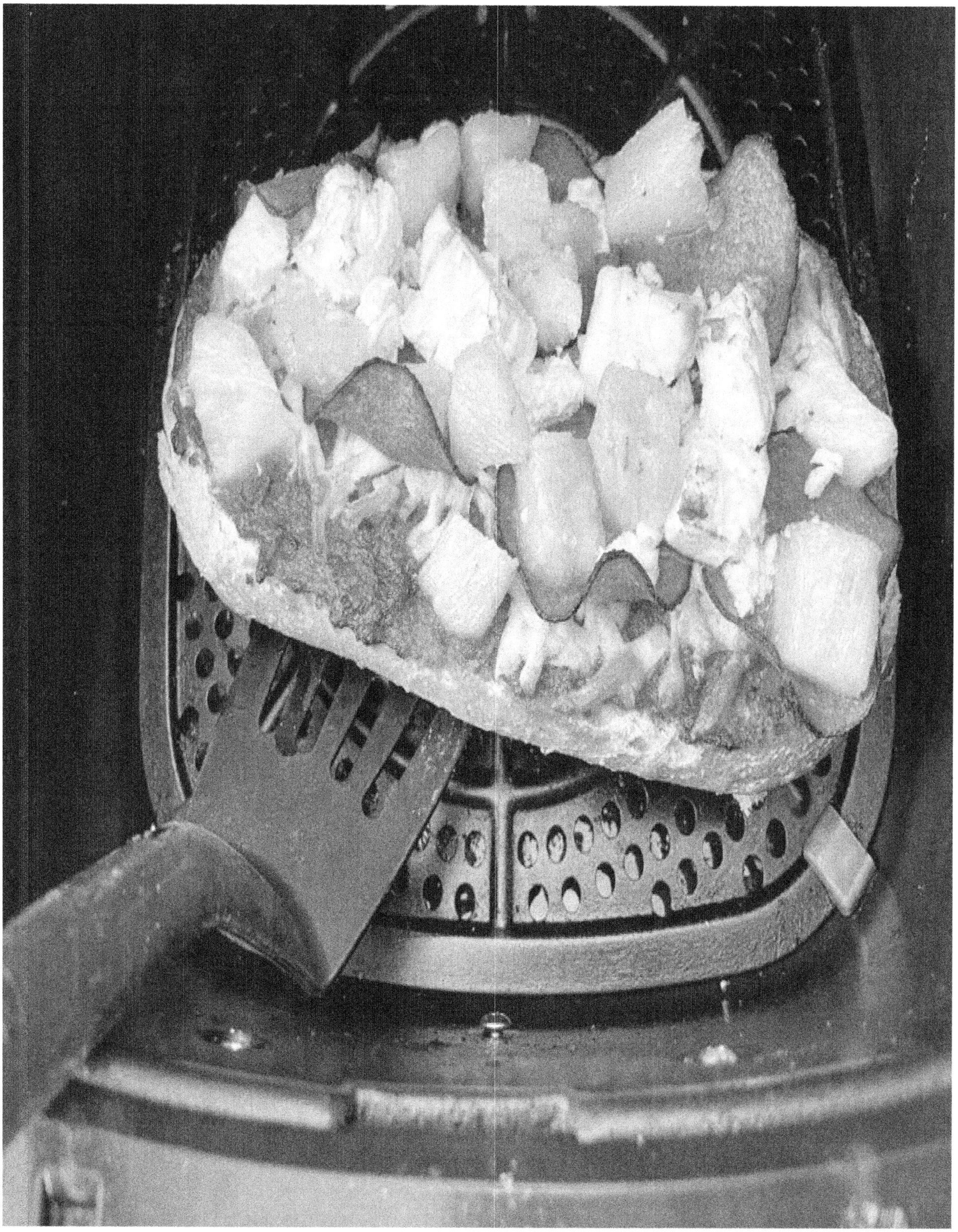

PART FOUR
SIDES AND VEGETABLES
1. AIR FRYER ASPARAGUS

Ingredients:

- 1 pound asparagus, trimmed and washed

- 1 tablespoon olive oil

- Salt and pepper, to taste

- Lemon zest, to taste (optional)

- Fresh lemon juice, to taste (optional)

Instructions:

● Set the air fryer to 400°F.

● In a large bowl, toss the asparagus with olive oil, salt, pepper, lemon zest (if using), and lemon juice (if using).

● Arrange the asparagus in the air fryer basket in a single layer.

● Cook for 10-12 minutes, flipping the asparagus halfway through, until tender and crisp.

● Serve immediately with your preferred dipping sauce.

Nutritional Information (per serving): Serving size: 1/4 of the recipe

- Calories: 80

- Total Fat: 7g

- Saturated Fat: 1g

- Trans Fat: 0g

- Cholesterol: 0mg

- Sodium: 210mg

- Total Carbohydrates: 6g

- Dietary Fiber: 3g

- Sugars: 2g

- Protein: 4g

- Vitamin A: 20%

- Vitamin C: 20

- Calcium: 4%

- Iron: 8%

2. AIR FRYER BAKED SWEET POTATOES

Ingredients:

- 2 medium sweet potatoes, peeled and cut into 1-inch cubes

- 1 tablespoon olive oil

- 1 teaspoon salt

- 1 teaspoon black pepper

- 1 teaspoon garlic powder

- 1 teaspoon paprika

- 1/2 teaspoon cumin

Instructions:

- Preheat the air fryer to 400°F.

- In a large bowl, combine the sweet potato cubes, olive oil, salt, pepper, garlic powder, paprika, and cumin.

- Toss to evenly coat the sweet potatoes.

- Transfer the sweet potatoes to the air fryer basket in a single layer.

- Cook for 15 minutes, flipping the sweet potatoes halfway through.

- Serve hot and enjoy.

Nutritional Information (per serving, assumes 2 servings):

- Saturated Fat: 1 g

- Cholesterol: 0 mg

- Sodium: 730 mg

- Total Carbohydrates: 30 g

- Dietary Fiber: 4 g

- Calories: 200

- Total Fat: 8 g

- Sugar: 6 g

- Protein: 2 g

3. AIR FRYER CARROT FRIES

Ingredients:

- 2 large carrots, peeled and sliced into thin fries

- 2 tbsp olive oil

- 1 tsp garlic powder

- 1 tsp dried thyme

- 1 tsp dried basil

- 1 tsp salt

- 1 tsp black pepper

Instructions:

- Preheat the air fryer to 400°F.

- In a bowl, mix together the sliced carrots, olive oil, garlic powder, thyme, basil, salt, and pepper.

- Move the carrots that have been seasoned to the air fryer basket.

- Cook for 15 minutes, flipping the carrots every 5 minutes until they are tender and crispy.

- Serve the carrots immediately, with your favorite dipping sauce, if desired.

Nutritional Information (per serving, based on 4 servings):

- Protein: 1g

- Carbohydrates: 11g

- Fiber: 2g

- Calories: 140

- Fat: 11g

- Saturated Fat: 2g

- Cholesterol: 0mg

- Sodium: 550mg

- Sugar: 4g

4. AIR FRYER CAULIFLOWER RICE

Ingredients:

- 1 large head of cauliflower, roughly chopped

- 1 tablespoon olive oil

- Salt and pepper, to taste

- Optional: garlic powder, dried herbs, or other seasonings of your choice

Instructions:

- Rinse the cauliflower and remove any leaves and stems. Chop it into small florets.

- Place the cauliflower florets into a food processor and pulse until it resembles rice. If you don't have a food processor, you can also grate the cauliflower on a box grater.

- In a bowl, mix the cauliflower rice with olive oil and any seasonings of your choice.

- Transfer the cauliflower rice to the air fryer basket and spread it out evenly.

- Cook at 400°F for 8-10 minutes or until the cauliflower is tender and slightly golden brown. Stir the rice every 4-5 minutes for even cooking.

- Season with additional salt and pepper to taste and serve hot as a side dish or as a base for stir-fries and other dishes.

Nutritional Information (per serving): Serves 4

- Dietary Fiber: 2g

- Calories: 75

- Total Fat: 7g

- Total Carbohydrates: 5g

- Sugars: 2g

- Protein: 3g

- Saturated Fat: 1g

- Cholesterol: 0mg

- Sodium: 35mg

5. AIR FRYER CORN ON THE COB

Ingredients:

- Four ears of corn, with husks, removed

- 1 tablespoon melted butter or oil

- Salt and pepper to taste

Instructions

- Preheat your air fryer to 400°F.

- Brush each ear of corn with melted butter or oil and sprinkle with salt and pepper.

- Place the ears of corn in the basket of the air fryer in a single layer, making sure not to overcrowd the basket.

- Cook for 10 to 15 minutes, flipping the corn halfway through cooking time until it is tender and lightly charred in spots.

- Remove the corn from the air fryer and serve with additional butter or oil, if desired.

Nutritional Information (per ear of corn):

- Calories: 60

- Fat: 4 g

- Sodium: 25 mg

- Carbohydrates: 8 g

- Fiber: 2 g

- Protein: 2 g

6. AIR FRYER GARLIC ROASTED POTATOES

Ingredients:

- 2 pounds baby potatoes, washed and dried

- 3 tablespoons olive oil

- 3 cloves garlic, minced

- 1 teaspoon salt

- 1/2 teaspoon black pepper

- 1 teaspoon dried rosemary

- 1 teaspoon dried thyme

Instructions:

• Cut the potatoes into bite-sized pieces, about 1 inch in size.

• In a large mixing bowl, add the potatoes and toss them with olive oil, garlic, salt, pepper, rosemary, and thyme.

• Set the air fryer to 400°F.

• Add the seasoned potatoes to the air fryer basket in a single layer, leaving some space between each piece.

• Cook for 20-25 minutes, flipping the potatoes halfway through the cooking time until they are tender and crispy on the outside.

• Serve the garlic-roasted potatoes hot, garnished with freshly chopped parsley if desired.

Nutritional Information (per serving, based on 4 servings):

- Saturated Fat: 2 g

- Fiber: 3 g

- Sugar: 2 g

- Protein: 3 g

- Cholesterol: 0 mg

- Sodium: 669 mg

- Carbohydrates: 26 g

- Calories: 239

- Fat: 14 g

7. AIR FRYER GRILLED VEGETABLES

Ingredients:

- One eggplant, sliced into rounds, cut into large pieces

- 1 large red bell pepper, sliced into strips

- 1 large yellow onion, sliced into rounds

- 2 large zucchinis, sliced into rounds

- 4 large garlic cloves, minced

- 2 tbsp olive oil

- Salt and pepper, to taste

- Fresh herbs such as basil, oregano, or parsley for garnish (this is optional)

Instructions:

- Preheat the air fryer to 400°F (200°C) for 5 minutes.

- In a large bowl, combine the eggplant, bell pepper, onion, zucchini, garlic, olive oil, salt, and pepper. Toss well to coat the vegetables evenly.

- Arrange the vegetables in a single layer in the air fryer basket. Make sure not to overcrowd the basket.

- Cook the vegetables for 10 minutes, flipping them once halfway through cooking.

- After 10 minutes, remove the basket from the air fryer and check the vegetables. If they're not yet tender, continue cooking for another 2-3 minutes or until they reach the desired tenderness.

- Serve the grilled vegetables hot, garnished with fresh herbs if desired.

Nutritional Information (Per Serving, Based on 4 Servings):

- Sodium: 109mg

- Total Carbohydrates: 10.2g

- Dietary Fiber: 3.5g

- Calories: 126

- Total Fat: 10.3g

- Saturated Fat: 1.5g

- Sugar: 4.9g

- Protein: 2.5g

- Cholesterol: 0mg

8. AIR FRYER MAC AND CHEESE BITES

Ingredients:

- Two cups of macaroni, cooked and drained

- 2 cups cheddar cheese, shredded

- 1/2 cup all-purpose flour

- 1 cup whole milk

- 1 large egg

- 1 tsp salt

- 1 tsp black pepper

- 1 cup Panko breadcrumbs

Instructions:

- In a large bowl, mix together the cooked macaroni and cheddar cheese.

- In a separate bowl, whisk together the flour, milk, egg, salt, and pepper.

- Pour the mixture over the macaroni and cheese and stir to combine.

- In a shallow dish, spread out the Panko breadcrumbs.

- Using a cookie scoop or spoon, form the mac and cheese mixture into 1-2 inch balls.

- Roll each ball in the Panko breadcrumbs, making sure to coat it evenly.

- Place the coated balls in a single layer in the air fryer basket, leaving a little space in between each one.

- Set the air fryer to 400°F and cook for 7-8 minutes, or until the outside is crispy and golden brown.

- Enjoy the dish straight away, with your preferred dipping sauce.

Nutritional Information (per serving, based on 12 servings):

- Total Carbohydrates: 19 g

- Dietary Fiber: 1 g

- Sugars: 1 g

- Protein: 12 g

- Calories: 245

- Total Fat: 13 g

- Saturated Fat: 7 g

- Cholesterol: 58 mg

- Sodium: 598 mg

9. AIR FRYER PARMESAN ROASTED BROCCOLI

Ingredients:

- 1 large head of broccoli, cut into florets

- 2 tablespoons olive oil

- 1/4 cup grated parmesan cheese

- 1/2 teaspoon garlic powder

- 1/2 teaspoon salt

- 1/4 teaspoon black pepper

Instructions:

- Set your air fryer to 400°F (200°C).

- In a large bowl, mix together the broccoli florets, olive oil, parmesan cheese, garlic powder, salt, and black pepper until the broccoli is evenly coated.

- Transfer the coated broccoli to the basket of the air fryer. Spread it out in a single layer, making sure that the florets are not crowded and there is plenty of space between them.

- Place the basket in the air fryer and cook for 12-15 minutes, until the broccoli is tender and the edges are golden brown.

- Once the cooking is complete, remove the basket from the air fryer and serve the parmesan roasted broccoli immediately.

Nutritional Information: Serving size: 1 cup

- Calories: 140

- Fat: 11g

- Saturated Fat: 3g

- Cholesterol: 8mg

- Sodium: 430mg

- Carbohydrates: 9g

- Fiber: 4g

- Sugar: 3g

- Protein: 6g

10. AIR FRYER POTATO WEDGES

Ingredients:

- 4 large potatoes, washed and cut into wedges

- 2 tablespoons olive oil

- 1 teaspoon salt

- 1 teaspoon black pepper

- 1 teaspoon garlic powder

- 1 teaspoon paprika

Instructions:

- In a large bowl, combine the potato wedges, olive oil, salt, pepper, garlic powder, and paprika. Coat the potatoes evenly by tossing them.

- Preheat the air fryer to 400°F for about 5 minutes.

- Place the potato wedges in the basket of the air fryer in a single layer, making sure not to overcrowd the basket.

- Cook for 20-25 minutes, flipping the wedges halfway through the cooking time until the potatoes are crispy and golden brown.

- Serve immediately with your preferred dipping sauce.

Nutritional Information per Serving (based on 4 servings):

- Carbohydrates: 28g

- Protein: 4g

- Calories: 200

- Fat: 9g

- Sodium: 630mg

11. AIR FRYER ROASTED BUTTERNUT SQUASH

Ingredients:

- 1 medium-sized butternut squash, peeled and chopped into 1-inch cubes

- 2 tbsp olive oil

- 1 tsp salt

- 1 tsp black pepper

- 1 tsp garlic powder

- 1 tsp dried thyme

Instructions:

- Turn the air fryer to 400°F (200°C).

- In a large bowl, combine the chopped butternut squash, olive oil, salt, pepper, garlic powder, and dried thyme. Toss to evenly coat the squash.

- Place the butternut squash in the air fryer basket in a single layer.

- Cook for 15-20 minutes, flipping halfway through, or until the squash is tender and lightly browned on the outside.

- Serve immediately, garnished with fresh herbs or a sprinkle of grated Parmesan cheese, if desired.

Nutritional Information (per serving, based on 4 servings):

- Cholesterol: 0mg

- Sodium: 600mg

- Carbohydrates: 14g

- Calories: 130

- Fat: 9g

- Fiber: 3g

- Sugar: 4g

- Protein: 2g

- Saturated Fat: 1g

12. AIR FRYER ROASTED CARROTS

- Calories: 95   - Fat: 7g   - Saturated Fat: 1g   - Cholesterol: 0mg

Ingredients:

- 1 pound carrots, peeled and cut into 1-inch pieces

- 1 tablespoon olive oil

- 1 teaspoon dried thyme

- Salt and pepper, to taste

Instructions:

- Set the air fryer to 400°F.

- In a large bowl, toss the carrots with olive oil, dried thyme, salt, and pepper until evenly coated.

- Now, arrange the carrots in the air fryer basket in a single layer.

- Cook for 20-25 minutes, flipping the carrots once halfway through, until tender and slightly caramelized.

- Serve hot as a side dish.

Nutritional Information (per serving, based on 4 servings):

- Sodium: 144mg

- Carbohydrates: 9g

- Fiber: 3g

- Sugar: 4g

- Protein: 1g

13. AIR FRYER ROASTED EGGPLANT

Ingredients:

- 1 large eggplant, sliced into 1/2-inch rounds

- 2 tablespoons olive oil

- Salt and pepper to taste

- 1 tablespoon dried basil

- 1 tablespoon dried oregano

Instructions:

- Preheat your air fryer to 400°F.

- Place the sliced eggplant in a large bowl.

- Add olive oil, salt, pepper, basil, and oregano to the bowl and mix well.

- Place the eggplant rounds in a single layer in the air fryer basket.

- Cook the eggplant for 10-12 minutes, flipping halfway through until they are tender and slightly charred.

- Serve immediately as a side dish or as a topping for sandwiches or salads.

Nutritional Information (per serving, based on 4 servings):

- Calories: 120

- Fat: 10g

- Saturated Fat: 1.5g

- Cholesterol: 0mg

- Sodium: 130mg

- Carbohydrates: 8g

- Fiber: 3g

- Sugar: 4g

- Protein: 2g

14. AIR FRYER ROASTED GARLIC

Ingredients:

- 1 head of garlic

- 1 teaspoon olive oil

- Salt and pepper, to taste

Instructions:

- Preheat your air fryer to 400°F.

- Cut the top off the head of the garlic to expose the individual cloves.

- Place the garlic head in the center of a piece of aluminum foil.

- Drizzle olive oil over the exposed cloves and sprinkle with salt and pepper.

- Wrap the garlic head tightly in the aluminum foil, creating a sealed packet.

- Place the packet in the air fryer basket and cook for 20-25 minutes, or until the garlic is tender and fragrant.

- Remove the garlic from the air fryer and let it cool for a few minutes.

- Squeeze the individual cloves from the skin and enjoy them as a spread on bread, as a topping for roasted meats, or added to sauces and soups.

Nutritional Information (per serving size of 1 clove):

- Fat: 0.3g

- Saturated Fat: 0.1g

- Cholesterol: 0mg

- Sodium: 1mg

- Protein: 0.2g

- Carbohydrates: 0.8g

- Fiber: 0.1g

- Calories: 4

- Sugar: 0.1g

15. AIR FRYER ROASTED GREEN BEANS

- Calories: 80

- Protein: 3g   - Sodium: 480mg

Ingredients:

- 1 lb green beans, trimmed

- 1 tbsp olive oil

- 1 tsp salt

- 1 tsp black pepper

- 1 tsp garlic powder

- 1 tsp paprika

Instructions:

● Preheat your air fryer to 400°F.

● In a large bowl, combine the green beans, olive oil, salt, pepper, garlic powder, and paprika. Toss until the green beans are evenly coated.

● Place the green beans in a single layer in the air fryer basket.

● Cook for 12-15 minutes, or until the green beans are tender and lightly browned, flipping them halfway through cooking.

● Remove the green beans from the air fryer and serve hot.

Nutritional Information (per serving, assuming 4 servings):

- Fat: 5g

- Carbohydrates: 8g

16. AIR FRYER SWEET POTATO COINS

Ingredients:

- 2 medium-sized sweet potatoes, peeled and sliced into 1/4-inch rounds

- 2 tablespoons of olive oil

- 1 teaspoon of salt

- 1/2 teaspoon of black pepper

- 1 teaspoon of paprika

- 1 teaspoon of garlic powder

Instructions:

- Preheat your air fryer to 400°F.

- In a large mixing bowl, add the sliced sweet potatoes, olive oil, salt, pepper, paprika, and garlic powder.

- Toss everything together until the sweet potatoes are evenly coated.

- Place the sweet potato rounds in a single layer in the air fryer basket.

- Cook for 15-20 minutes, flipping once halfway through until they are tender and golden brown.

- Serve hot as a side dish or snack.

Nutritional Information (per serving, assumes 4 servings):

- Sodium: 553 mg

- Carbohydrates: 18 g

- Fiber: 3 g

- Sugar: 4 g

- Protein: 2 g

- Calories: 153

- Fat: 9 g

- Saturated Fat: 1 g

- Cholesterol: 0 mg

17. AIR FRYER TATER TOTS

Ingredients:

- 2 large russet potatoes, peeled and grated

- 1/4 cup all-purpose flour

- 1/2 teaspoon salt

- 1/4 teaspoon black pepper

- Non-stick cooking spray

Instructions:

- Turn your air fryer to 400°F (200°C).

- In a large bowl, combine the grated potatoes, flour, salt, and pepper. Mix well.

- Using your hands, form the mixture into small, cylindrical tater tot shapes.

- Place the tater tots in the air fryer basket and spray lightly with non-stick cooking spray.

- Cook for 15-20 minutes, flipping the tater tots halfway through until they are crispy and golden brown.

- Serve warm with a dipping sauce of your choice.

- Servings: 4-6

Nutritional Information per serving (based on 6 servings):

- Cholesterol: 0mg

- Sodium: 380mg

- Protein: 4g

- Total Carbohydrates: 29g

- Dietary Fiber: 2g

- Sugars: 1g

- Calories: 150

- Total Fat: 2g

- Saturated Fat: 0g

- Trans Fat: 0g

18. AIR FRYER TWICE BAKED POTATOES

Ingredients:

- 4 medium-sized potatoes

- 4 tablespoons of unsalted butter

- 1/2 cup of sour cream

- 1/2 cup of grated cheddar cheese

- 2 cloves of garlic, minced

- Salt and pepper, to taste

- Fresh chives or green onions, chopped (optional)

Instructions:

- Scrub the potatoes clean and poke them several times with a fork.

- Place the potatoes in the air fryer basket and cook at 400°F for 30-35 minutes, or until fully cooked and tender.

- Remove the potatoes from the air fryer and let them cool for 5-10 minutes.

- Cut the potatoes in half lengthwise and scoop out the flesh, leaving about a 1/4 inch border of potato skin.

- In a bowl, mash the potato flesh together with the butter, sour cream, grated cheese, minced garlic, salt, and pepper.

- Spoon the mixture back into the potato skins, mounding it slightly.

- Return the stuffed potatoes back to the air fryer basket and cook at 400°F for an additional 10-15 minutes, or until the cheese is melted and the edges are golden brown.

- Garnish with chopped fresh chives or green onions, if desired.

- Serving size: 2 potatoes

Nutritional Information (per serving):

- Calories: 392

- Fat: 25g

- Carbohydrates: 35g

- Protein: 8g

- Sodium: 212mg

- Cholesterol: 56mg

19. AIR FRYER ZUCCHINI CHIPS

Ingredients:

- 2 medium zucchinis, sliced into 1/4 inch rounds
- 1/2 cup all-purpose flour
- 1/2 teaspoon garlic powder
- 1/2 teaspoon onion powder
- 1/2 teaspoon dried basil
- 1/2 teaspoon dried oregano
- 1/2 teaspoon paprika
- 1/2 teaspoon salt
- 1/4 teaspoon black pepper
- 2 large eggs, beaten
- 1 cup panko breadcrumbs
- Cooking spray or olive oil spray

Instructions:

- Turn your air fryer to 400°F (205°C) for 5 minutes.
- In a shallow dish, mix together the flour, garlic powder, onion powder, basil, oregano, paprika, salt, and pepper. Beat the eggs in a shallow bowl. Place the panko breadcrumbs in a separate shallow dish.
- Dip each zucchini slice into the flour mixture, then the egg mixture, and finally the panko breadcrumbs.
- Lightly coat each slice with cooking spray or olive oil spray.
- Place the breaded zucchini slices in the air fryer basket in a single layer, making sure not to overlap them.
- Cook for 8-10 minutes or until the zucchini chips are golden brown and crispy, flipping once halfway through.
- You can serve it immediately with your preferred dipping sauce.

Nutritional Information (per serving, based on 8 servings):

- Cholesterol: 55 mg
- Caloric intake: 113 Kcal
- Fat: 3 g
- Sodium: 587 mg
- Carbohydrates: 17 g
- Fiber: 2 g
- Sugar: 4 g
- Protein: 5 g

20. AIR FRYER ROASTED CAULIFLOWER

Ingredients:

- 1 head of cauliflower, cut into florets

- 2 tablespoons olive oil

- 1 teaspoon salt

- 1 teaspoon black pepper

- 1 teaspoon garlic powder

- 1 teaspoon dried thyme

- 1 teaspoon dried basil

Instructions:

- Set the air fryer to 400°F (200°C).

- In a large bowl, mix the cauliflower florets with olive oil, salt, pepper, garlic powder, thyme, and basil.

- Transfer the seasoned cauliflower to the air fryer basket, making sure the florets are in a single layer and not overcrowded.

- Cook in the preheated air fryer for 15 to 20 minutes or until the cauliflower is tender and browned on the outside.

- Rotate the basket halfway through the cooking process in order to guarantee even cooking.

- Once cooked, remove the roasted cauliflower from the air fryer and serve hot.

Nutritional Information (per serving, based on 4 servings):

- Cholesterol: 0 mg

- Sodium: 706 mg

- Protein: 3 g

- Total Carbohydrates: 8 g

- Dietary Fiber: 3 g

- Calories: 123

- Total Fat: 10 g

- Saturated Fat: 1.5 g

- Sugars: 3 g

AIR FRYER COOKBOOK FOR BEGINNERS

PART FIVE

DESSERTS

1. AIR FRYER APPLE CHIPS

Ingredients:

- 2 medium apples, sliced

- 1 tsp lemon juice

- 1 tsp cinnamon

- 1 tbsp granulated sugar

- Pinch of salt

Instructions:

• Slice the apples into thin rounds using a mandoline slicer or a sharp knife. If the slices are thin, the chips will be crisp.

• In a large bowl, mix together the lemon juice, cinnamon, sugar, and salt.

• Add the apple slices to the bowl and toss to coat evenly with the mixture.

• Set the air fryer to 400°F.

• Arrange the apple slices in a single layer in the air fryer basket, making sure they don't overlap.

• Cook for 8-10 minutes, flipping the apple slices halfway through cooking until the edges are golden brown and the centers are crispy.

• Remove from the air fryer and let cool for a few minutes before serving. Serve warm.

Nutritional Information (per serving, 1 medium apple)

- Fat: 0g

- Carbohydrates: 16g

- Calories: 60

- Fiber: 3g

- Protein: 1g

- Sodium: 30m

2. AIR FRYER APPLE PIE BITES

Ingredients:

- 1 medium peeled and chopped apple

- 2 teaspoons sugar

- 1 teaspoon ground cinnamon

- A quarter teaspoon of nutmeg

- 1/4 teaspoon salt 1 tablespoon melted butter 1 beaten egg

- One refrigerated pie crust sheet

Instructions:

- Set your air fryer to 400 degrees Fahrenheit (200 degrees Celsius).

- On a lightly floured board, roll out the pie crust.

- Combine the diced apples, sugar, cinnamon, nutmeg, salt, melted butter, and beaten egg in a mixing bowl. Mix until everything is properly blended.

- Cut the pie crust into 2-inch circles using a cookie cutter.

- Fill each pie dough circle with a tablespoon of the apple mixture.

- Fold the spherical pie crust in half, closing the corners and forming a half-moon shape.

- Brush the remaining beaten egg over the tops of the apple pie bits.

- Cook for 10-12 minutes, or until the crust is golden brown, in the air fryer basket with the apple pie bits.

- If preferred, serve warm with a dollop of vanilla ice cream.

Nutritional Information (per serving, based on 6 servings):

- Cholesterol: 36 mg

- Sodium: 243 mg

- Carbohydrates: 20 g

- Fiber: 1 g

- Sugar: 9 g

- Protein: 2 g

- Calories: 168

- Fat: 9 g

- Saturated Fat: 4 g

3. AIR FRYER BANANA BREAD

Ingredients:

- 1 cup all-purpose flour

- 1 tsp baking powder

- 1/4 tsp baking soda

- 1/4 tsp salt

- 1/2 cup granulated sugar

- 1/3 cup melted unsalted butter

- 2 large ripe bananas, mashed

- 1 large egg

- 1 tsp pure vanilla extract

Instructions:

- In your medium bowl, whisk together the flour, baking powder, baking soda, and salt.

- In a large bowl, whisk together the melted butter, mashed bananas, egg, and vanilla extract.

- Gradually add the dry ingredients to the wet ingredients, mixing until just combined. Do not overmix.

- Pour the batter into a greased and floured 6-inch round cake pan.

- Place the pan in the air fryer basket and set the temperature to 330°F. Cook for 25-30 minutes, or until a toothpick inserted into the center of the bread comes out clean.

- Let the bread cool for 10 minutes before removing it from the pan and slicing. Serve warm with butter or your favorite spread.

Nutritional Information (per slice, based on 8 slices per loaf):

- Carbohydrates: 36g

- Protein: 3g

- Sugar: 18g

- Calories: 250

- Fat: 12g

- Sodium: 140mg

4. AIR FRYER BLUEBERRY MUFFINS

Ingredients:

- 1 1/2 cups all-purpose flour

- 1/2 cup granulated sugar

- 2 teaspoons baking powder

- 1/4 teaspoon salt

- 1 large egg

- 1/2 cup milk

- 1/4 cup melted unsalted butter

- 1 teaspoon vanilla extract

- 1 cup fresh blueberries

Instructions:

• In your large mixing bowl, whisk together the flour, sugar, baking powder, and salt.

• In another bowl, beat together the egg, milk, melted butter, and vanilla extract until well combined.

• Pour the wet ingredients into the dry ingredients and mix until just combined. Do not overmix.

• Now, what you will do is carefully fold in the blueberries and pour the batter into a muffin tin lined with muffin cups or lightly greased with cooking spray.

• Place the muffin tin in the air fryer basket and set the temperature to 375°F.

• Cook for 15-18 minutes or until a toothpick inserted into the center of a muffin comes out clean.

• Remove the muffin tin from the air fryer and let the muffins cool for 5 minutes before serving.

Nutritional Information (per muffin):

- Sodium: 150mg

- Carbohydrates: 28g

- Calories: 200

- Fat: 9g

- Saturated Fat: 5g

- Cholesterol: 40mg

- Fiber: 1g

- Sugar: 15g

- Protein: 3g

5. AIR FRYER BROWNIES

Ingredients:

- 1/2 cup unsalted butter, melted

- 1 teaspoon baking powder

- 1/4 teaspoon salt

- 1 cup granulated sugar

- 1/2 cup semisweet chocolate chips

- 2 large eggs

- 1 teaspoon vanilla extract

- Half a cup of unsweetened cocoa powder.

- One cup of all-purpose flour

Instructions:

- In a medium mixing bowl, combine the flour, cocoa powder, baking powder, and salt. Stir until well mixed.

- In your large mixing bowl, beat together the sugar, melted butter, eggs, and vanilla extract until smooth.

- Gradually add the dry ingredients to the wet mixture and mix until just combined. Stir in the chocolate chips.

- Pour the batter into a greased and floured air fryer-safe dish, such as a cake pan or a springform pan, and spread evenly.

- Place the dish in the air fryer basket and cook at 350°F for 18-20 minutes, or until a toothpick inserted into the center comes out clean.

- Remove from the air fryer and let cool for 5-10 minutes before slicing and serving.

Nutritional Information (per serving, based on 16 servings):

- Sodium: 60mg

- Carbohydrates: 22g

- Fiber: 2g

- Sugar: 16g

- Protein: 3g

- Calories: 200

- Fat: 13g

- Saturated Fat: 7g

- Cholesterol: 50mg

6. AIR FRYER CARROT CAKE

Ingredients:

- 1 1/2 cups all-purpose flour

- 1 teaspoon baking powder

- 1 teaspoon baking soda

- 1 teaspoon ground cinnamon

- 1/2 teaspoon ground ginger

- 1/2 teaspoon ground nutmeg

- 1/2 teaspoon salt

- 1 1/2 cups granulated sugar

- 1/2 cup vegetable oil

- 3 large eggs

- 2 teaspoons vanilla extract

- 1/2 cup unsweetened applesauce

- 1/2 cup chopped walnuts (optional)

- 1/2 cup raisins (optional)

- Two cups grated carrots (about 4 medium carrots)

- 1/2 cup cream cheese frosting (for serving)

Instructions:

- In your medium bowl, whisk together the flour, baking powder, baking soda, cinnamon, ginger, nutmeg, and salt.

- In a large bowl, beat together the sugar, oil, eggs, and vanilla extract until well combined.

- Mix the wet ingredients together, then slowly incorporate the dry ingredients, stirring until just incorporated.

- Fold in the grated carrots, applesauce, chopped walnuts (if using), and raisins (if using).

- Put the greased 9-inch round cake pan on a flat surface and pour the batter into it.

- Place the pan in the air fryer basket and air fry at 330°F for 25-30 minutes, or until a toothpick inserted into the center comes out clean.

- Let the cake cool completely, then spread the cream cheese frosting on top before serving.

Nutritional Information (per serving, without frosting, based on 12 servings):

- Cholesterol: 40 mg

- Sodium: 210 mg

- Carbohydrates: 37 g

- Fiber: 1 g

- Protein: 3 g

- Sugar: 25 g

- Calories: 260

- Fat: 12 g   - Saturated Fat: 1 g

7. AIR FRYER CINNAMON ROLLS

Ingredients:

- 1 can refrigerated cinnamon rolls (8 counts)

- Cooking spray

Instructions:

- Set your air fryer to 350°F (175°C).

- Coat the air fryer basket with cooking spray.

- Place the cinnamon rolls in the air fryer basket, leaving some space between them.

- Cook the cinnamon rolls in the air fryer for 8-10 minutes, or until they are golden brown on the outside and cooked through on the inside.

- Remove the cinnamon rolls from the air fryer basket and let them cool for a few minutes.

- Frost the cinnamon rolls with the included frosting or make your own frosting.

Nutritional Information (per serving, based on 1 cinnamon roll with frosting):

- Cholesterol: 0mg

- Sodium: 420mg

- Carbohydrates: 25g

- Fiber: 0g

- Calories: 160

- Fat: 6g

- Saturated Fat: 2g   - Sugars: 12g   - Protein: 2g

8. AIR FRYER FRUIT TARTS

Ingredients:

- 1 package refrigerated pie crusts (2 count)

- 1/2 cup fruit preserves (such as apricot or raspberry)

- 2 cups mixed fresh fruit (such as berries, sliced peaches, or sliced kiwi)

- 1 tablespoon granulated sugar

- 1 tablespoon cornstarch

- Cooking spray

- Powdered sugar for dusting (optional)

Instructions:

- Turn your air fryer to 375°F (190°C).

- On a floured surface, roll out each pie crust to about 1/8 inch thickness.

- Cut each pie crust into four equal pieces, making a total of eight pieces.

- Coat the air fryer basket with cooking spray.

- Place the pie crust pieces in the air fryer basket, leaving some space between them.

- Cook the pie crust pieces in the air fryer for 6-8 minutes, or until they are golden brown and crispy.

- While the pie crust pieces are cooking, mix together the fruit preserves, sugar, and cornstarch in a small saucepan.

- Heat the fruit preserve mixture over low heat, stirring occasionally, until it is smooth and slightly thickened.

- Remove the pie crust pieces from the air fryer basket and let them cool for a few minutes.

- Spread a spoonful of the fruit preserve mixture on each pie crust piece.

- Top each pie crust piece with a mixture of fresh fruit.

- If desired, dust the fruit tarts with powdered sugar before serving.

Nutritional Information (per serving, based on 1 fruit tart):

- Sugars: 16g

- Fat: 10g

- Saturated Fat: 4g

- Cholesterol: 0mg

- Calories: 240

- Sodium: 170mg

- Carbohydrates: 36g

- Fiber: 2g

- Protein: 2g

9. AIR FRYER FUNNEL CAKES

Ingredients:

- 1 cup all-purpose flour

- 1 teaspoon baking powder

- 1/4 teaspoon salt

- 1 egg

- 1/2 cup milk

- 1/4 cup granulated sugar

- 1 teaspoon vanilla extract

- Cooking spray

- Powdered sugar for dusting

Instructions:

- Turn your air fryer to 375°F (190°C).

- In your medium mixing bowl, whisk together the flour, baking powder, and salt.

- In a separate mixing bowl, whisk together the egg, milk, sugar, and vanilla extract until well combined.

- Add the dry ingredients to the wet ingredients and stir until a smooth batter forms.

- Here you coat the air fryer basket with cooking spray.

- Pour the funnel cake batter into a squeeze bottle or a large reseal-able plastic bag with one corner cut off.

- Squeeze the batter into the air fryer basket in a circular motion, making a spiral shape.

- Cook the funnel cake in the air fryer for 4-6 minutes, or until it is golden brown and crispy on the outside.

- Use tongs to carefully remove the funnel cake from the air fryer basket and transfer it to a plate.

- Dust the funnel cake with powdered sugar before serving.

Nutritional Information (per serving, based on 1 funnel cake):

- Cholesterol: 70mg

- Sodium: 390mg

- Carbohydrates: 74g

- Calories: 350

- Fat: 4g

- Saturated Fat: 1g

- Fiber: 1g

- Sugars: 34g

- Protein: 7g

10. AIR FRYER GRILLED PEACHES

Ingredients:

- 4 ripe peaches, halved and pitted

- 2 tablespoons olive oil

- 2 tablespoons honey

- 1/2 teaspoon cinnamon

- Pinch of salt

- Cooking spray

Instructions:

- Turn your air fryer to 375°F (190°C).

- In a small mixing bowl, whisk together the olive oil, honey, cinnamon, and salt.

- Now, coat the air fryer basket with cooking spray.

- Brush the cut sides of the peach halves with the honey mixture.

- Place the peach halves in the air fryer basket, and cut the side down.

- Cook the peaches in the air fryer for 6-8 minutes, or until they are tender and slightly caramelized.

- Remove the peaches from the air fryer basket and let them cool for a few minutes before serving.

Nutritional Information (per serving, based on 1 grilled peach half):

- Sodium: 10mg

- Carbohydrates: 14g

- Fiber: 1g

- Sugars: 13g

- Protein: 1g

- Fat: 4g

- Saturated Fat: 0.5g

- Calories: 90

- Cholesterol: 0mg

11. AIR FRYER POUND CAKE

Ingredients:

- 1 1/2 cups all-purpose flour

- 1/2 teaspoon baking powder

- 1/2 teaspoon salt

- 1/2 cup unsalted butter, softened

- 1 cup granulated sugar

- 2 large eggs

- 1 teaspoon vanilla extract

- 1/2 cup milk

- Cooking spray

Instructions:

- Preheat your air fryer to 320°F (160°C).

- In your medium mixing bowl, whisk together the flour, baking powder, and salt.

- In a separate mixing bowl, cream the butter and sugar together using an electric mixer until light and fluffy.

- Add the eggs to the mixture one at a time, stirring after each addition. Lastly, add the vanilla extract and mix it in.

- Gradually add the dry ingredients to the wet ingredients, alternating with the milk and mixing until just combined.

- Spray a 6-inch baking pan with cooking spray and pour the pound cake batter into the pan.

- Place the pan in the air fryer basket and cook the pound cake for 35-40 minutes, or until a toothpick inserted into the center comes out clean.

- Use tongs to carefully remove the baking pan from the air fryer and let the pound cake cool for a few minutes before slicing and serving.

Nutritional Information (per serving, based on 1/8th of the pound cake):

- Cholesterol: 75mg

- Sodium: 180mg

- Calories: 280

- Carbohydrates: 39g

- Fiber: 0g

- Sugars: 25g

- Protein: 3g

- Fat: 12g

- Saturated Fat: 7g

AIR FRYER COOKBOOK FOR BEGINNERS

12. AIR FRYER PUMPKIN MUFFINS

Ingredients:

- 1 1/2 cups all-purpose flour

- 1 teaspoon baking powder

- 1/2 teaspoon baking soda

- 1/2 teaspoon salt

- 1 teaspoon ground cinnamon

- 1/2 teaspoon ground ginger

- 1/4 teaspoon ground nutmeg

- 1/4 teaspoon ground cloves

- 1 cup canned pumpkin puree

- 1/2 cup granulated sugar

- 1/4 cup vegetable oil

- 2 large eggs

- 1 teaspoon vanilla extract

- Cooking spray

Instructions:

- Preheat your air fryer to 320°F (160°C).

- In a medium mixing bowl, whisk together the flour, baking powder, baking soda, salt, cinnamon, ginger, nutmeg, and cloves.

- In a separate mixing bowl, whisk together the pumpkin puree, sugar, vegetable oil, eggs, and vanilla extract until well combined.

- Mix the dry ingredients together, then slowly incorporate them into the wet ingredients, stirring until everything is thoroughly blended.

- Spray a muffin tin with cooking spray and divide the pumpkin muffin batter evenly among the 12 cups.

- Place the muffin tin in the air fryer basket and cook the muffins for 15-20 minutes, or until a toothpick inserted into the center comes out clean.

- Use tongs to carefully remove the muffin tin from the air fryer and let the muffins cool for a few minutes before removing them from the tin.

Nutritional Information (per serving, based on 1 muffin):

- Calories: 130

- Fat: 5g

- Saturated Fat: 1g

- Cholesterol: 30mg

- Sodium: 170mg

- Carbohydrates: 19g

- Fiber: 1g

- Sugars: 8g

- Protein: 2g

13. AIR FRYER S'MORES

Ingredients:

- 6 graham cracker sheets, broken into halves

- 6 large marshmallows

- 3 oz milk chocolate, broken into small pieces

Instructions:

- Set your air fryer to 400°F (200°C).

- Place half of the graham cracker sheets in the air fryer basket and top each one with a piece of milk chocolate.

- Cut each marshmallow in half horizontally and place one half on top of each chocolate-covered graham cracker.

- Place the air fryer basket in the preheated air fryer and cook the s'mores for 2-3 minutes, or until the marshmallows are golden brown and slightly melted.

- Remove the basket from the air fryer and top each marshmallow with the remaining graham cracker halves.

- Serve the s'mores immediately while still warm.

Nutritional Information (per serving, based on 1 s'more):

- Calories: 140

- Carbohydrates: 23g

- Fiber: 1g

- Sugars: 14g

- Protein: 2g

- Fat: 5g

- Saturated Fat: 3g

- Cholesterol: 0mg

- Sodium: 80mg

14. AIR FRYER STRAWBERRY TURNOVERS

Ingredients:

- 1 sheet puff pastry, thawed

- 1/2 cup diced strawberries

- 2 tablespoons granulated sugar

- 1/2 teaspoon cornstarch

- 1/2 teaspoon vanilla extract

- 1 large egg

- 1 tablespoon water

- Powdered sugar (optional)

Instructions:

- Turn your air fryer to 375°F (190°C).

- In a small mixing bowl, combine the diced strawberries, sugar, cornstarch, and vanilla extract.

- On a lightly floured surface, roll out the puff pastry into a rectangle and cut it into 4 equal squares.

- Spoon the strawberry filling onto one-half of each square, leaving a small border around the edge.

- Fold the other half of the puff pastry over the filling and use a fork to crimp the edges together.

- In a small bowl, whisk together the egg and water to create an egg wash.

- Brush the tops of each turnover with the egg wash.

- Place the turnovers in the air fryer basket and cook for 10-12 minutes, or until they are golden brown and puffed up.

- Remove the turnovers from the air fryer and let them cool for a few minutes before dusting them with powdered sugar (if desired).

Nutritional Information (per turnover):

- Sodium: 157mg

- Carbohydrates: 25g

- Fiber: 1g

- Sugars: 6g

- Protein: 4g

- Fat: 17g

- Calories: 270

- Saturated Fat: 5g

- Cholesterol: 41mg

15. AIR FRYER SWEET POTATO PIE

Ingredients:

- 1 pre-made pie crust
- 2 cups mashed sweet potato
- 1/2 cup brown sugar
- 2 eggs
- 1/2 cup evaporated milk
- 1 teaspoon ground cinnamon
- 1/2 teaspoon ground nutmeg
- 1/4 teaspoon salt
- 1/4 cup melted butter
- 1 teaspoon vanilla extract

Instructions:

- Turn your air fryer to 350°F (175°C).
- Roll out the pie crust and place it in a 9-inch pie dish.
- In your large bowl, mix together the mashed sweet potato, brown sugar, eggs, evaporated milk, cinnamon, nutmeg, salt, melted butter, and vanilla extract. Stir until everything is combined.
- Pour the sweet potato mixture into the pie crust and smooth it out with a spatula.
- Place the pie dish in the air fryer basket and cook for 30-35 minutes, or until the filling is set and the crust is golden brown.
- Remove the pie from the air fryer and let it cool to room temperature before serving.

Nutritional Information (per slice, based on 8 slices):

- Sodium: 291mg
- Carbohydrates: 42g
- Calories: 311
- Fat: 14g
- Saturated Fat: 7g
- Cholesterol: 73mg
- Fiber: 2g
- Sugars: 24g
- Protein: 5g

16. AIR FRYER VANILLA CUPCAKES

Ingredients:

- 1 cup all-purpose flour

- 3/4 teaspoon baking powder

- 1/4 teaspoon baking soda

- 1/4 teaspoon salt

- 1/2 cup granulated sugar

- 1/4 cup unsalted butter, softened

- 1 large egg

- 1/2 cup milk

- 1 teaspoon vanilla extract

Instructions:

- Preheat your air fryer to 320°F (160°C).

- In a medium mixing bowl, whisk together the flour, baking powder, baking soda, and salt.

- In a separate large mixing bowl, cream together the sugar and butter until light and fluffy.

- Beat in the egg until well combined.

- Gradually stir in the dry ingredients, alternating with the milk and vanilla extract, until the batter is smooth.

- Place cupcake liners in a muffin tin and fill each liner about 2/3 full with the cupcake batter.

- Place the muffin tin in the air fryer basket and cook for 12-15 minutes, or until a toothpick inserted into the center of a cupcake comes out clean.

- Remove the muffin tin from the air fryer and let the cupcakes cool completely before frosting.

Nutritional Information (per cupcake, without frosting):

- Cholesterol: 35mg

- Sodium: 99mg

- Protein: 2g

- Carbohydrates: 21g

- Fiber: 0.4g

- Calories: 146

- Fat: 6g

- Saturated Fat: 3.5g

- Sugars: 11g

17. AIR FRYER WAFFLE BITES

Ingredients:

- 1 cup all-purpose flour

- 2 teaspoons baking powder

- 1/4 teaspoon salt

- 1/4 cup granulated sugar

- 1 large egg

- 1 cup milk

- 2 tablespoons unsalted butter, melted

- 1 teaspoon vanilla extract

Instructions:

- Preheat your air fryer to 360°F (182°C).

- In a medium mixing bowl, whisk together the flour, baking powder, salt, and sugar.

- In a separate large mixing bowl, whisk together the egg, milk, melted butter, and vanilla extract.

- Gradually stir in the dry ingredients until the batter is smooth and well combined.

- Lightly spray the waffle iron with nonstick cooking spray and pour a small amount of batter into each waffle mold.

- Cook the waffles in the air fryer for 4-5 minutes, or until golden brown and crispy.

- Carefully remove the waffles from the waffle iron and cut them into bite-sized pieces.

Nutritional Information (per serving, based on 4 servings):

- Cholesterol: 64mg

- Sodium: 347mg

- Carbohydrates: 32g

- Protein: 6g

- Fiber: 1g

- Sugars: 10g

- Calories: 212

- Fat: 7g

- Saturated Fat: 4g

18. AIR FRYER WARM CINNAMON APPLES

Ingredients:

- 3 medium-sized apples, peeled, cored, and sliced

- 2 tablespoons unsalted butter, melted

- 1 tablespoon brown sugar

- 1 teaspoon ground cinnamon

- 1/4 teaspoon ground nutmeg

- Pinch of salt

Instructions:

- Turn your air fryer to 375°F (190°C).

- In a small mixing bowl, whisk together the melted butter, brown sugar, cinnamon, nutmeg, and salt.

- Add the sliced apples to the mixture and toss until they are well coated.

- Place the coated apples in the air fryer basket and cook for 8-10 minutes, shaking the basket occasionally, until the apples are soft and tender.

- Serve the warm cinnamon apples as a delicious dessert or snack.

Nutritional Information (per serving, based on 3 servings):

- Sodium: 52mg

- Carbohydrates: 22g

- Fiber: 3g

- Sugars: 17g

- Protein: 0g

- Calories: 132

- Fat: 6g

- Saturated Fat: 4g

- Cholesterol: 15mg

19. AIR FRYER YEAST DONUTS

Ingredients:

- 1/2 cup warm milk (110-115°F)

- 2 1/4 tablespoons dry active yeast

- 1 tablespoon granulated sugar

- 1 large egg

- 2 teaspoons melted unsalted butter

- 1 teaspoon of salt

- 2 1/2 cups regular flour

- Nonstick cooking spray

- Dust with 1/4 cup powdered sugar

Instructions:

- Combine the warmed milk and active dry yeast in a small bowl. Allow the mixture to settle for 5 minutes to allow the yeast to activate.

- Whisk together the granulated sugar, egg, melted butter, and salt in a large mixing bowl.

- Stir the yeast mixture into the big mixing basin to blend.

- Mix in the flour gradually until the mixture comes together and is smooth.

- Now, here you knead the dough for 5-7 minutes on a floured surface, or until it turns elastic.

- Form the dough into a ball and set it aside in an oiled bowl, covered with a clean cloth or plastic wrap. Allow it to rise for 1 hour.

- Set your air fryer to 350°F (175°C).

- Roll out the dough until it's approximately 1/2 inch thick on a floured surface. To make donut shapes, use a donut cutter or a circular cookie cutter.

- Spray the air fryer basket lightly with nonstick cooking spray and lay the doughnuts in the basket, leaving enough space between them.

- Cook the donuts in the air fryer for 5-6 minutes, turning halfway through, until golden brown.

- Let the donuts cool slightly before dusting them with powdered sugar and serving.

Nutritional Information (per serving, based on 12 servings):

- Cholesterol: 21mg - Sodium: 104mg - Carbohydrates: 28g

- Fiber: 1g

- Sugars: 8g

- Protein: 3g

- Calories: 154

- Fat: 3g

- Saturated Fat: 2g

20. AIR FRYER ZUCCHINI BREAD

Ingredients:

- 1 1/2 cups all-purpose flour

- 1 teaspoon baking powder

- 1/2 teaspoon baking soda

- 1/2 teaspoon salt

- 1 teaspoon ground cinnamon

- 1/2 teaspoon ground nutmeg

- 2 eggs

- 1/2 cup vegetable oil

- 3/4 cup granulated sugar

- 1 teaspoon vanilla extract

- 1 cup shredded zucchini

- Nonstick cooking spray

Instructions:

- Preheat your air fryer to 300°F (150°C).

- In a medium mixing bowl, whisk together the flour, baking powder, baking soda, salt, cinnamon, and nutmeg.

- In a separate mixing bowl, beat the eggs, then mix in the vegetable oil, granulated sugar, and vanilla extract.

- Combine the wet and dry ingredients and mix until everything is evenly incorporated.

- Fold in the shredded zucchini until it's evenly distributed in the batter.

- Lightly spray a 7-inch cake pan with nonstick cooking spray and pour the batter into the pan.

- Place the pan in the air fryer basket and air fry for 50-55 minutes, or until a toothpick inserted into the center of the bread comes out clean.

- Remove the pan from the air fryer and let it cool for 10 minutes before removing the bread from the pan and slicing.

Nutritional Information (per serving, based on 8 servings):

- Cholesterol: 47mg

- Sodium: 234mg

- Carbohydrates: 30g

- Fiber: 1g

- Calories: 255

- Fat: 14g

- Saturated Fat: 1g

- Sugars: 16g

- Protein: 3g

LARISSA H. BARTON

PART SIX
TIPS FOR COOKING WITH AN AIR FRYER

Cooking with an air fryer may be a fun and exciting experience, but there are a few techniques you can do to improve the quality of your meals. Here are some air fryer cooking techniques to help you get the most out of this versatile equipment.

- **Warm the Air Fryer:** Just like you should preheat your oven before baking, you should preheat your air fryer before cooking. This guarantees that your food cooks evenly and that it does not cling to the basket.

- **Shake It Up.** To guarantee that your food cooks evenly, shake the basket every now and then. This will help to disperse your food and prevent it from sticking to the basket or cooking unevenly.

- Cooking spray can help prevent your food from sticking to the basket and allow it to cook more evenly. Just apply a little coating to prevent your meal from becoming greasy.

- Overcrowding the basket can restrict hot air from circulating over your food, resulting in uneven cooking. Allow enough room for your meal to cook evenly.

- Cooking times may vary depending on the kind and quantity of food you're cooking, as well as the air fryer you're using. Keep an eye on your meal while it cooks and adjusts the time accordingly.

- **Keep an Eye on the Temperature.** The temperature of your air fryer may also affect the amount of time it takes to cook. Check the temperature on a regular basis and adjust as required.

- **Use a Meat Thermometer.** Having a meat thermometer is crucial for making sure that your meat has been cooked to the correct temperature. This will assist to avoid undercooked or overcooked meat.

- **Cook Food in Batches.** To guarantee consistent cooking and to save time, try cooking your food in batches. Simply shake the basket and adjust the cooking time between batches as required.

TROUBLESHOOTING COMMON AIR FRYER ISSUES

Cooking with an air fryer might be a wonderful experience, but it is not without flaws. Here are some of the most typical air fryer issues, as well as troubleshooting tips:

- Whenever your food is clinging to the basket, it might be due to a shortage of cooking spray or an overloading of the basket. Use a little layer of cooking spray and allow your meal plenty of room to cook evenly.

- **Uneven Cooking:** It might be due to overcrowding, not shaking the basket sufficiently, or failing to adjust the cooking time. Allow adequate room for your meal, shake the basket often, and adjust cooking time as required.

- **Food Cooking Too Slowly:** If your food is taking longer to cook than intended, it might be because the air fryer was not warmed or the temperature was set too low. Preheat your air fryer and keep an eye on the temperature.

- **Overcooking Food:** Whenever your food is overcooking, it might be because the temperature is too high or the cooking period is too lengthy. Make any necessary adjustments to the temperature and cooking time.

- **Basket Not Fitting Properly:** If the basket in your air fryer isn't fitting properly, it might be due to food or oil accumulation. To avoid this problem, clean the basket and air fryer on a regular basis.

- **Smoky or Burning Smell:** This might be because food has spilled over the heating element. To avoid this problem, keep the air fryer clean on a regular basis.

- **If your air fryer isn't turning on,** it might be due to a power outage or a problem with the heating element. If the problem continues, check the power supply and contact the manufacturer for help.

- You can fix common air fryer difficulties and continue to enjoy delicious and healthy meals by following these recommendations. If you continue to have problems with your air fryer, please contact the manufacturer for help.

- **If your food isn't crisping up,** this could be due to a lack of cooking spray, overflowing the basket, or cooking at a low temperature. Use a little layer of cooking spray, allow your meal plenty of room, and adjust the temperature as required.

- **Excessive Oil or Fat:** If your food is still excessively oily or fatty, it might be because you didn't drain extra oil or fat, used too much cooking spray, or used the incorrect sort of oil. Drain excess oil and fat, apply a little layer of cooking spray, and use oils with a high smoke point.

- **Basket Warping:** If your basket is warping, it might be due to overheating or putting metal utensils in it. Use plastic or silicone utensils in the basket and avoid exposing it to high heat.

- **If your air fryer is creating a lot of noise,** it might be due to a loose or cracked fan blade. If the problem continues, inspect the fan blades and contact the manufacturer for help.

- **Leaking Air Fryer:** If your air fryer is leaking, it might be due to a faulty seal or a heating element issue. If the problem continues, inspect the seal and contact the manufacturer for help.

HOW TO CLEAN AND MAINTAIN YOUR AIR FRYER

Cleaning and maintaining your air fryer is essential to ensuring its longevity and ensuring that you always have the best cooking results. Here are some tips for cleaning and maintaining your air fryer:

- **Allow it to cool down:** Before you start cleaning your air fryer, make sure it has cooled down completely. This will help to avoid any unintentional burns or injuries.

- **Clean the basket and tray:** The basket and tray are the parts of the air fryer that come into direct contact with your food. They should be cleaned after each use. Clean the items with warm, sudsy water and a gentle sponge or cloth. If there is any stubborn food residue, try soaking the parts in warm water for a few minutes before cleaning.

- **Wipe down the exterior:** Wipe down the exterior of your air fryer with a damp cloth to remove any fingerprints or spills.

- **Avoid harsh chemicals:** Avoid using harsh chemicals or abrasive materials when cleaning your air fryer. This can damage the surface and potentially cause harm to you and your food.

- **Store it properly:** When you're not using your air fryer, store it in a cool, dry place. Do not store it near heat sources or in moist environments, as this can damage the unit.

- **Regularly check for wear and tear:** Over time, parts of your air fryer may wear out or become damaged. Regularly inspect your air fryer for any damage, and contact the manufacturer if you need any replacement parts.

LARISSA H. BARTON

CONCLUSION
PERSONAL REFLECTION

As the author of "Air Fryer Cookbook for Beginners," I can tell that the experience of writing this book has been a truly rewarding one. I've always been interested in cooking and discovering the versatility of the air fryer has only fueled that interest.

I was skeptical of air fryers when I first heard about them. How could a machine that fries food with hot air produce the same crisp, delicious results as traditional deep frying? But when I tried it for myself, I was completely blown away. The air fryer not only produced delicious, crispy results, but it also did so in a healthier and more convenient manner. As I experimented with various recipes, I realized how versatile the air fryer could be. The air fryer can prepare everything from main dishes and sides to appetizers and desserts. It worked especially well for delicate things like fish and vegetables, which may be difficult to cook uniformly in a typical oven.

But, as much as I like the air fryer, I recognized that there were many others out there who were put off by this new kitchen device. That is why I created the "Air Fryer Cookbook for Beginners." I wanted to make it as simple as possible for people to understand how the air fryer works and how to use it to prepare wonderful, nutritious meals. I got the chance to share some of my favorite recipes as well as some tips and methods that I've learned along the way while writing this book. I hope this book inspires others to get creative in the kitchen and embrace this incredible appliance. Whether you're a seasoned chef or just starting out, the air fryer is a great tool for quickly preparing delicious, healthy meals.

MEAL PLAN

15 DAYS MEAL PLAN

A 15-Day Air Fryer Meal Plan for Healthy and Delicious Eating

Day 1:

- **Breakfast:** Air Fryer Bacon and Eggs

- **Lunch:** Air Fryer Grilled Cheese Sandwich with Tomato Soup

- **Dinner:** Air Fryer Pork Chops with Roasted Potatoes and Carrots

Day 2:

- **Breakfast:** Air Fryer Cinnamon Sugar Donuts

- **Lunch:** Air Fryer Chicken Caesar Salad

- **Dinner:** Air Fryer Shrimp Scampi with Zucchini Noodles

Day 3:

- **Breakfast:** Air Fryer Breakfast Burrito with Salsa

- **Lunch:** Air Fryer Veggie and Hummus Wrap

- **Dinner:** Air Fryer Fish and Chips with Coleslaw

Day 4:

- **Breakfast:** Air Fryer French Toast Sticks
- **Lunch:** Air Fryer Buffalo Cauliflower Bites with Blue Cheese Dip
- **Dinner:** Air Fryer Beef and Broccoli Stir Fry with Rice

Day 5:

- **Breakfast:** Air Fryer Sausage and Cheese Breakfast Sliders
- **Lunch:** Air Fryer BBQ Chicken Sandwich with Sweet Potato Fries
- **Dinner:** Air Fryer Grilled Chicken with Sweet Potato Mash and Green Beans

Day 6:

- **Breakfast:** Air Fryer Cinnamon Sugar Monkey Bread
- **Lunch:** Air Fryer Veggie and Tofu Skewers with Rice
- **Dinner:** Air Fryer Steak Fajitas with Guacamole and Salsa

Day 7:

- **Breakfast:** Air Fryer Veggie and Cheese Omelette
- **Lunch:** Air Fryer Turkey Club Sandwich with Sweet Potato Chips
- **Dinner:** Air Fryer Lemon and Herb Baked Salmon with Asparagus

Day 8:

- **Breakfast:** Air Fryer Apple and Cinnamon Waffles
- **Lunch:** Air Fryer Thai Peanut Chicken Wraps
- **Dinner:** Air Fryer BBQ Ribs with Mac and Cheese

Day 9:

- **Breakfast:** Air Fryer Breakfast Sausage and Hashbrown Casserole
- **Lunch:** Air Fryer Greek Salad with Grilled Chicken
- **Dinner:** Air Fryer Stuffed Bell Peppers with Rice and Ground Beef

Day 10:

- **Breakfast:** Air Fryer Blueberry Muffins
- **Lunch:** Air Fryer Chicken Quesadillas with Salsa
- **Dinner:** Air Fryer Pork Tenderloin with Garlic Butter Roasted Potatoes and Carrots

Day 11:

- **Breakfast:** Air Fryer Avocado Toast with Fried Egg

- **Lunch:** Air Fryer Veggie and Pesto Pizza

- **Dinner:** Air Fryer Beef and Mushroom Stir Fry with Rice

Day 12:

- **Breakfast:** Air Fryer French Toast Roll-Ups with Maple Syrup

- **Lunch:** Air Fryer Buffalo Chicken Wings with Blue Cheese Dip

- **Dinner:** Air Fryer Lemon and Herb Chicken with Roasted Asparagus

Day 13:

- **Breakfast:** Air Fryer Veggie and Cheese Quiche

- **Lunch:** Air Fryer Chicken and Broccoli Alfredo with Garlic Bread

- **Dinner:** Air Fryer Sizzling Steak Fajitas with Guacamole

Day 14:

- **Breakfast:** Air Fryer Peanut Butter and Jelly Muffins

- **Lunch:** Air Fryer Veggie and Hummus Pita Pockets

- **Dinner:** Air Fryer BBQ Chicken Thighs with Roasted Sweet Potatoes and Carrots

Day 15:

- **Breakfast:** Air Fryer Oatmeal Raisin Cookies

- **Lunch:** Air Fryer Grilled Veggie and Cheese Panini

- **Dinner:** Air Fryer Baked Cod with Garlic Butter and Roasted Pot

SAFETY TIPS FOR USING AN AIR FRYER

Using an air fryer is a convenient and healthy way to cook your favorite foods, but it's important to follow safety guidelines to prevent accidents and ensure safe cooking. Here are some safety tips for using an air fryer:

- **Read the manual** - Before using your air fryer, make sure to read the manual thoroughly to understand the functions and safety precautions of the device.

- **Avoid overloading** - Overloading the air fryer basket can cause the food to cook unevenly and also poses a risk of fire. Make sure to leave enough room between the foods for hot air to circulate.

- **Use heat-resistant utensils** - Always use heat-resistant utensils, such as silicone or metal tongs, when handling food in the air fryer basket. Avoid using plastic utensils as they may melt and contaminate the food.

- **Don't touch hot surfaces** - The exterior of the air fryer and the basket will get hot during cooking, so always use oven mitts or potholders to handle the device.

- **Be careful with liquids** - Avoid adding liquids, such as oil or sauce, directly to the bottom of the air fryer basket. Liquids can cause the heating element to short-circuit and create a fire hazard. Instead, use a cooking spray or brush to apply oil to the food.

- **Check the food regularly** - Air fryers cook food faster than traditional ovens, so check on your food regularly to prevent overcooking or burning.

- **Keep the air fryer clean** - Regularly cleaning your air fryer and removing any crumbs or debris from the bottom can prevent fires caused by overheating.

- **Unplug the device** - Always unplug the air fryer when not in use and never leave it unattended while cooking.

TIPS FOR SUBSTITUTING INGREDIENTS

Cooking with an air fryer may be a lot of fun, but you might not have all of the supplies on hand all of the time. Substituting items may be a fantastic way to explore new recipes and be creative in the kitchen, whether you're trying to satisfy dietary restrictions or just want to change things up. Here are some pointers to help you properly substitute components in air fryer recipes:

- **Understand the ingredient's function** - Before considering a substitute, evaluate the ingredient's purpose in the recipe. Some components, for example, may be utilized for taste, while others may be used to give moisture or structure.

- **Experiment with spices and herbs** - If you don't have a certain item, try adding flavor to your recipe using various spices or herbs. If a recipe asks for thyme and you don't have any, substitute rosemary or oregano.

- **Use dairy replacements** - If you're lactose sensitive or vegan, there are several dairy substitutes that may be used in air fryer recipes. Unsweetened almond milk or coconut milk, for example, may be used in place of cow's milk.

- If you have gluten sensitivity, consider using gluten-free flour when coating foods for the air fryer. Wheat flour substitutes include almond flour, coconut flour, and chickpea flour.

- Use oil substitutes - If you're trying to cut down on fat, you may use oil substitutes in your air fryer recipes. Instead of oil, try using low-fat cooking sprays or broth.

- Try different types of protein - If a recipe calls for chicken and you don't have any, try using a different type of protein, such as tofu, tempeh, or fish. Cooking time and temperature may need to be changed, so see the recipe for details.

- Experiment with different vegetables - If you don't have a specific vegetable called for in a recipe, try using a different vegetable that you do have on hand. If a recipe asks for carrots and you don't have any, substitute sweet potatoes or butternut squash.

GLOSSARY OF INGREDIENTS AND TERMS

Having a solid understanding of these ingredients and terms can greatly enhance the cooking experience and help to create delicious and well-rounded meals.

Here is a glossary of some commonly used ingredients and terms in air fryer cooking:

- Air Fryer Basket - The main cooking area in an air fryer where food is placed for cooking.

- Breadcrumbs - Usually made from dried bread, breadcrumbs are used to coat food items for added crunch and texture.

- Coating - A thin layer of breadcrumbs, flour, or egg mixture applied to food items to create a crispy outer layer during cooking.

- Dredging - The process of coating food items in flour, egg, and breadcrumbs before cooking.

- Marinade - A mixture of ingredients used to flavor and tenderize meat before cooking.

- Oil Mist - A spray bottle used to mist oil on food items before cooking in an air fryer.

- Panko Breadcrumbs - A type of Japanese breadcrumb that creates a crispier and lighter coating compared to traditional breadcrumbs.

- Rack - An accessory that can be placed in an air fryer basket to elevate food items and allow for more even cooking.

- Shake - The act of shaking or tossing food items in the air fryer basket during cooking to ensure even cooking and prevent sticking.

- Seasoning Blend - A combination of dried herbs and spices used to flavor food items.

- Tossing - The act of tossing or flipping food items in the air fryer basket during cooking to ensure even cooking and prevent sticking.

LARISSA H. BARTON

GLOSSARY OF COOKING TECHNIQUES

Knowing the right cooking techniques can elevate your meals and take them to the next level. In this section, we will provide a glossary of cooking techniques that you may come across while using your air fryer and cooking from this cookbook.

- **Baking:** Baking is a dry heat cooking technique that is typically used for cakes, pastries, bread, and other baked goods. It's achieved by cooking food in an oven, with the heat circulating around it, allowing for even cooking. In an air fryer, you can achieve the same result by cooking your food in a basket with hot air circulating around it.

- **Braising:** Braising is a moist-heat cooking technique that involves browning food in a small amount of fat before slowly cooking it in a covered pot with a liquid. This technique is great for cooking tough cuts of meat, as the long cooking time allows for the meat to become tender.

- **Broiling:** Broiling is a dry heat cooking technique that involves cooking food under direct heat. This is similar to grilling, but with the heat source coming from above the food, instead of below. In an air fryer, broiling can be achieved by setting the temperature to high and cooking food in the basket directly under the heating element.

- **Frying:** The cooking technique involves heating oil and then cooking food in it. Air frying is a healthier alternative to traditional frying, as it uses hot air instead of oil to cook food. This results in food that is crispy on the outside and tender on the inside, without the added fat.

- **Grilling:** Grilling is a dry heat cooking technique that involves cooking food over direct heat, typically from a grill or griddle. In an air fryer, grilling can be achieved by cooking food in the basket directly under the heating element.

- **Roasting:** Roasting is a dry heat cooking technique that involves cooking food in an oven or on a spit. In an air fryer, you can achieve the same result by cooking food in the basket with hot air circulating around it.

- **Steaming:** Steaming is a moist heat cooking technique that involves cooking food in a steamer basket above boiling water. In an air fryer, steaming can be achieved by using a steaming basket or adding a small amount of water to the bottom of the air fryer basket.

- **Stir-frying:** Stir-frying is a cooking technique that involves quickly cooking food in a wok or pan over high heat, while constantly stirring. In an air fryer, stir-frying can be achieved by cooking food in the basket and tossing it frequently to ensure even cooking.

Printed in Great Britain
by Amazon